Conchas y Café Zine
Vol. IX, Issue 2

Leading Lines

a DSTL arts publication

DSTL Arts presents

Leading Lines

Conchas y Café Zine

Vol. IX, Issue 2

Cover Design and Image: Abraham Jaramillo

Book Design: Abraham Jaramillo and Luis Antonio Pichardo

ISBN: 978-1-946081-74-2

10 9 8 7 6 5 4 3 2 1

www.DSTLArts.org

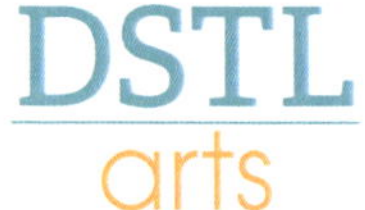

Los Angeles, CA

Contents

Conchas y Café Zine

Vol. IX, Issue 2

Leading Lines

Mentor

Clarissa Cervantes

"Mentor" celebrates all the great professors, instructors, and mentors that challenge students to learn, to grow, and to develop their own voices and skills. Mentors make the world a better place through their lenses, knowledge, and dedication.

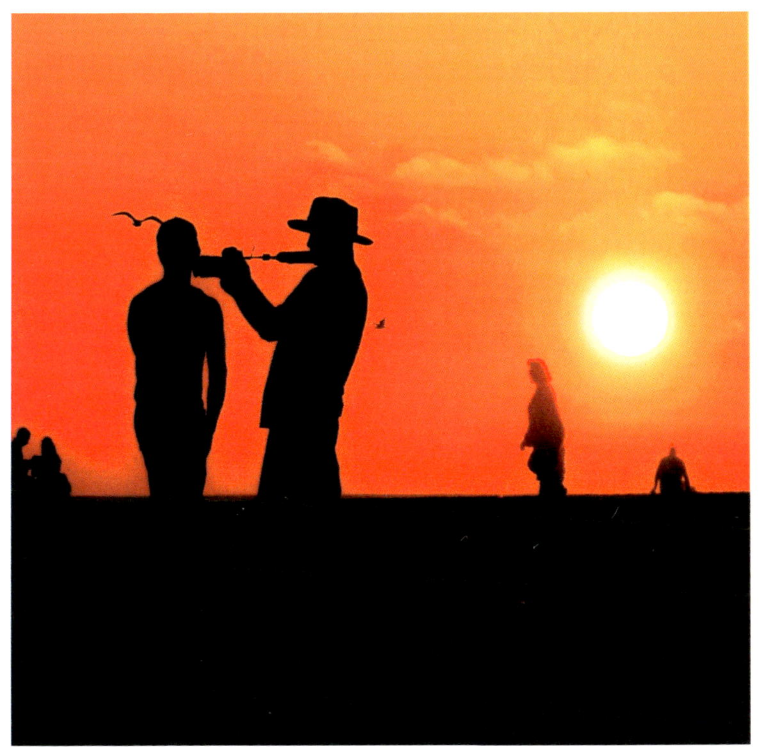

The New Couple in 5B by Lisa Unger

Alayna Abravanel

Act I

1) So, today I learned something new about the book, and it is originally like when you write on the book, and sometimes, you like to take notes on your Chromebook. Sometimes, when you write the book on any writing you would like to do, and write some stuff in the library, you like using your iPad and your Apple Pencil to write in your notebook too. I'm forgetting some new stuff that you really have. Study with me. You might have work and note-taking because talking to your friend is not an option.

2) Checking out a book at your local library is an option too, and taking good care of your hygiene is really important to know your identification and your manners. And sometimes, when it comes to writing your book, you're the new couple in 5B by Lisa Unger.

Act II

What are the characteristics of this story? When it comes to trust in your 1:1 aide and listening to what the teacher has to say, and not interrupting them when they are trying to say or speak, taking off your shoes is not allowed on school grounds–and you are never, ever allowed to take off your shoes and start counting the little kid's fingers and toes or I will tell my mom and your dad.

The Power of Now by Eckhart Tolle

Alayna Abravanel

Today, I will be studying "The Power of Now" by Eckhart Tolle, and sometimes it takes time to become a student or teacher. You will need your laptop, Apple Pencil, calculator, erasers, and sometimes, when it comes to your writing your thoughts, like how do you get better when you get sick and drink hot tea, who do you know? About being a part of a team: sometimes you get something, like a reward, like getting some new books. And that is all a day of me becoming a college student.

Writing on How Was Your Day Today

Alayna Abravanel

What did you do today? I went to the animal sanctuary today in Santa Clarita. What is something you can do to make a better place? Sometimes, like taking notes on your iPad and your Lenovo Chromebook Laptop, and sometimes when you get your grades up, it is like studying for your digital SAT premium.

On Fridays and Saturdays, I study to go to the school that I want to go to, and I hang out with my friends at the help group at L.A. City College. When you graduate from the college, you get a certificate from the school. When I was 18, I was in school.

By the time you are done with school, you can choose which jobs you want to get, and when the job says you can work at this company, then you can do anything you want to do when it comes to writing your thoughts, like your school assignments.

If it is school work or talking to your friends and being nice to one another and not fighting your classmates, that is not allowed on school grounds, and dating is against the school policy. If you cannot respect it, then I am sorry; but you can't date, and if you ask me again, then you will be kicked off from school and will never, ever come back again.

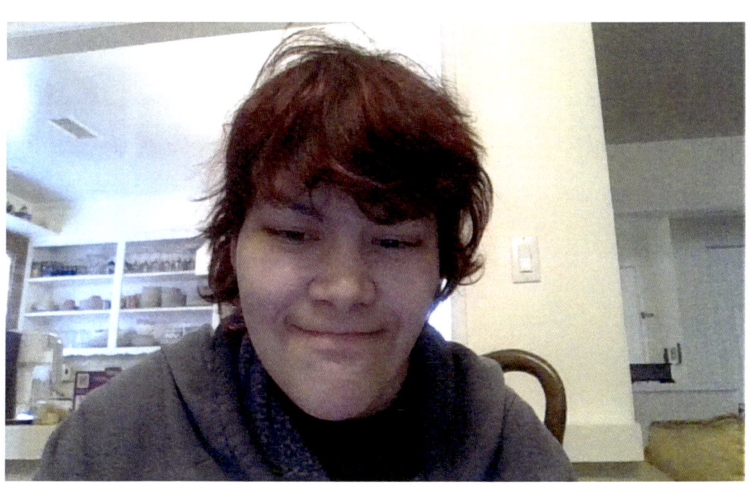

And the Storm Came In

Erica Castro

I am not surprised
The truth is like a storm unexpected
But absolutely overwhelming

I am human
So I feel and it hurts
It cuts me with a cheese grater

Because that is how infidelity is
It cuts me in tiny little pieces
Cuts me as I emotionally bleed

The truth that I thought was true
Was lies
And that damn storm came in and hit me

Cold water
All over my body hitting hitting
Hitting me with the lies of a double life

Society says this is what men do
This happens to everybody
She does not mean anything

I am the mother of his child
The irony
Is he claims he is a good father

How stupid to think
He can separate the relationship
With our child and that of his mother

Doesn't he know
You hurt the mother
You hurt the child

Secrets upon secrets
So long as nobody knows
It is okay

But what happens
When the storm comes in
And almost kills the mother
She questions her worth
Her motherhood
Her womanhood

All because the little boy
Inside him
Was like a child searching for his next toy

Dark Cup

Erica Castro

They say that we all have cup
And we chose for the cup to be full
Or empty
That happiness is a choice
And that life is what we make of it

Tell me then how do you fill a cup
When you are suffering never-ending grief
One year six months and your suicide
Stripped the hope I had for joy
And the empty dark cup became normal

Left with never-ending questions
What-ifs infect my mind
The emptiness of not having you near
And yet I have to still carry this empty cup
Still trying to live life

I will never feel the way you loved me
The way you brightened my life with your smile
My precious girl
How do you make sense of what is impossible

I will never know
why your cup was dark and empty
why you pretended it was full
why you chose to suffer alone
why I was not there for you

And today I carry a dark empty cup
Not because I want to die
But because I am grieving your loss
Angry at God
Angry at myself

Nobody seems to understand
I am not the same person
Your death has cut me to my core
I do not understand this grief
It feels like a life sentence
To carry around this empty dark cup

Because I will forever be living
With a missing piece
That died with you
And my cup will never have light
Or be full again because I lost you

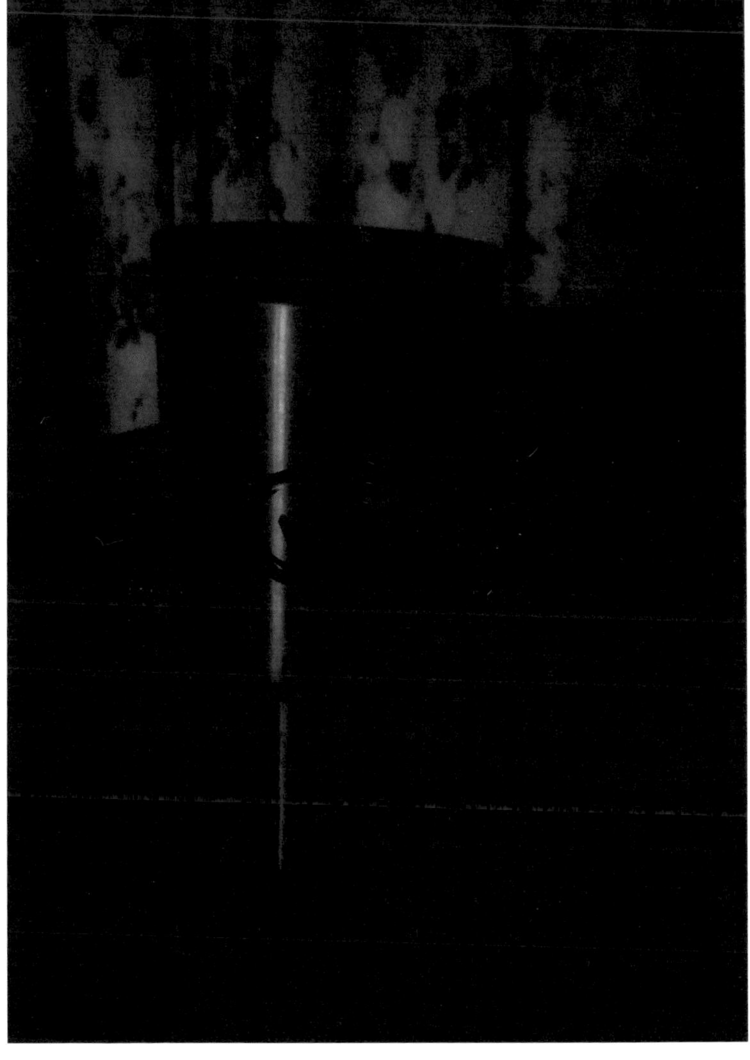

Cup in The Light

Erica Castro

HOB that is what it says
Meaning you had
A heart of beauty
That filled this world with your heart

Your compassion
And empathy brought hope
To those who needed love
You filled other people's cups

You believed in others
And breathed inspiration
In their lives
To this day although dead

You are bringing light to the world
To all the people you touched
To all the people you helped
To all the ones you healed

The way you loved us
The ones blessed enough
To be your family
Will always be remembered

We are forever grateful
For we had the privilege to watch you grow
Witness your little eccentricities
And your artistic ways
We saw how hard you worked

And yet it hurts
That you are gone
I need to remember the gifts
You left behind

And though everyday
I wish I could wrap
Myself around you
I was honored
to have known and loved you

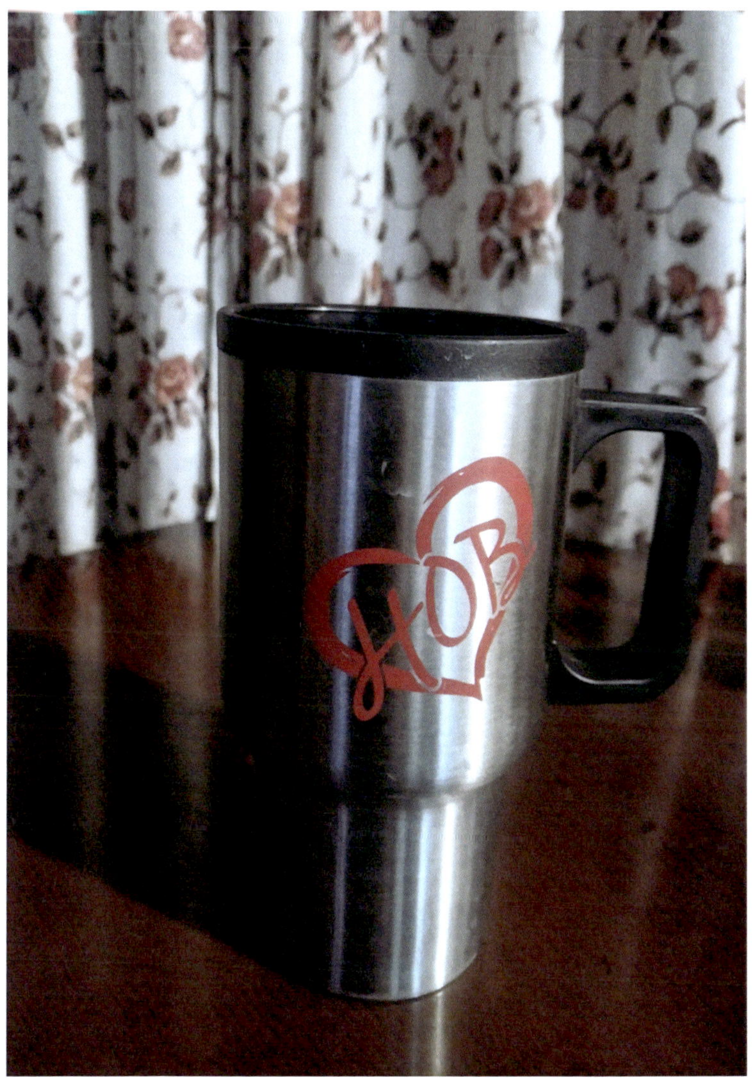

Boys Toys

Erica Castro

My entire life from the moment
I was born I didn't fit
I know my mother struggled
Being pregnant with 2 little boys
And dealing with my alcoholic father

I was awkward
Dying to be accepted
Mother dies
Raised by my brothers and father
Wearing boys clothes

Short hair
Playing football
Playing with cars
Playing video games
Playing with only boys

I wasn't normal
Tomboy
Just unofficially
One of the boys
Not sure how to relate to girls

I was different
Dead mother
Raised by men
Weird
Unacceptable

I lived the life
Of a misfit
Poetry showed me the way
My poetic family

Made me feel at home

But still the feelings
That came from toy cars
Being different

Often creep in
Unexpectedly

I question my worth
And if I fit
I try to remember
My poetic friend
Who love me

It is okay
To be different
It is okay to be weird
I was made for toy cars
I was made not to fit

Paper Dolls

Erica Castro

I used to play
With my mother

We'd dress the dolls
With paper clothes
Vintage outfits

I used to want to be like them
With their hippy clothes

Bell bottom pants
Flowered shirts
Lipstick

It would all end

These dolls would be trashed
As if they never existed

Cancer invaded my mother
Stripped her of her life

The last feminine thing
She showed me

Raised by a dad
Two brothers
I followed their lead

Lost what it meant
To be a girl

I remember

The smile on my mom's face
The joy of the pretty dolls

Today finding
Paper dolls do exist
Forty-nine-years old

Trying to relive that
Memory

Of a little five-year-old girl
Admiring her mother
Feeling loved
Dressing dolls

Hoping she could be one

Poeting

Erica Castro

I poet my grief
And scream
Maybe someone out there
Can hear me

I am not okay
I try to move through it
I can't it's too much
So I spill my hurt on the page

Maybe I am not alone
Through my words
Someone out there can see
Or listen and understand

This is what it's like to be me
I have moments of reprieve
Other times I'm on the floor
Crying wailing trying to catch my breath

I can't seem to control my grief
It comes in different moments
Different times
Almost always unexpectedly

And one more time
I become paralyzed
With grief
Wanting the world to stop

Yet I have to move
And move
And move
And move

I am seeing the world
Through a kaleidoscope
Distorted unclear
Confusing

Everyone around me
Is normal
Still living life
As if nothing has changed

I can't see clearly
Because this grief
Shows everything clouded
As if my eyes have cataracts

Grief devours me
So I poet my grief
And tell others
Your story

So that they know
To love
To care
To have compassion

Because we all need hope
So because of you
And the loss I suffered
I poet my grief

And tell the world
Love yourself enough
To speak your grief
And tell your truth

Mental health steals lives

A Random Second

Nery Martinez Jr.

Chaotic and orderly,
the way I like it,
Just as daily life.

A random second,
frozen in time,

imprinted in my mind,

Not quite a photographer,
But I can see the snapshot,
before it flies

away.

Chaotic and orderly,
the way I like it,
Just as daily life.

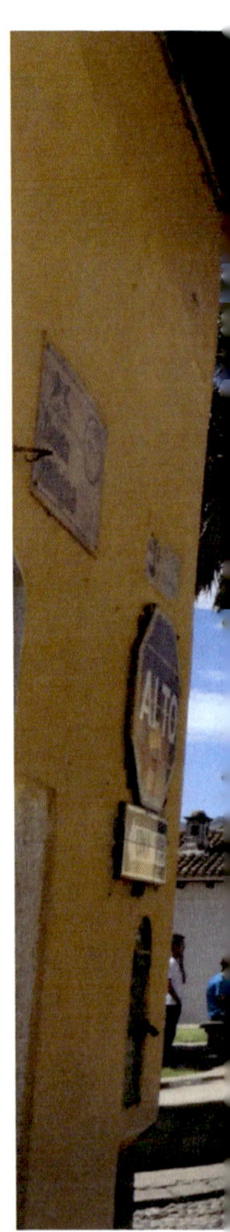

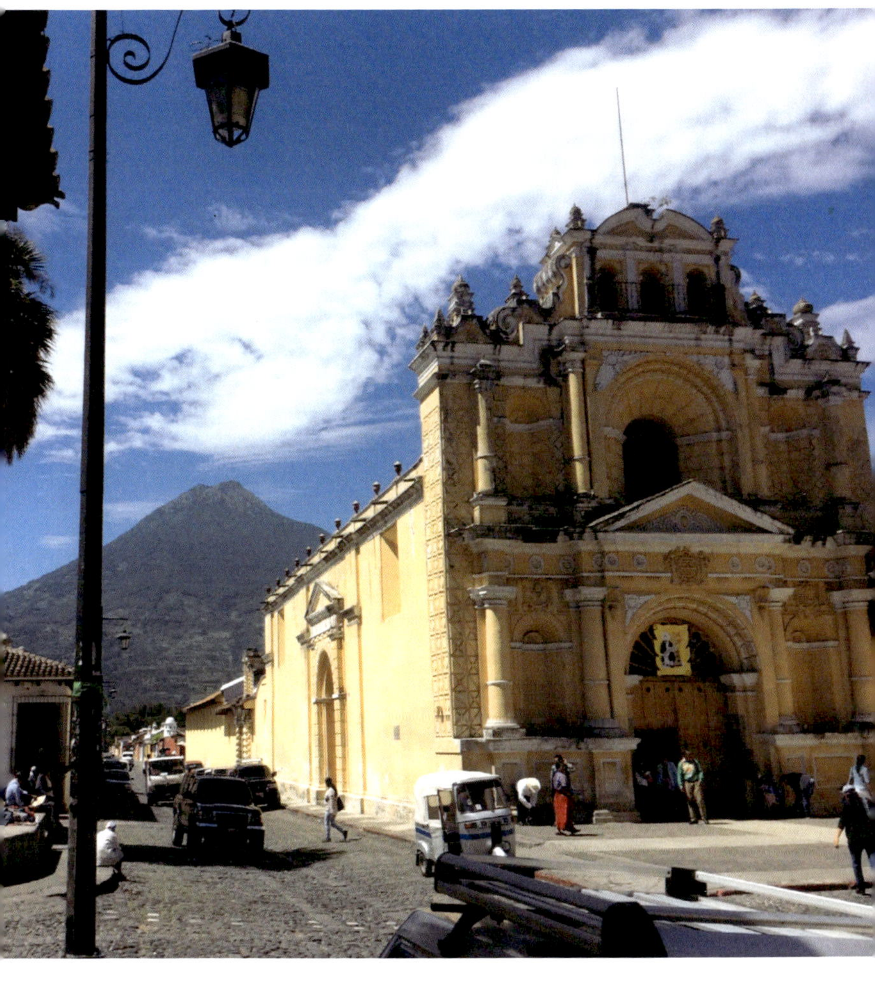

Conversation, Unhad

Nery Martinez Jr.

All the things I wanted to say,
Wanted you to know,

Half true, half a lie,

From a distance,
The awkwardness of silence,
The emptiness of us,

The coldness of 2 chairs and a table,

The distance is understandable.

Between us
secrets and weird glances
set us apart

So sad
so lonely
so together

and yet so far

In what instance, the empty table closes the gap?
Memories unbuilt,
A bond unfulfilled,
The oppression of nothingness,
The trust we never had.

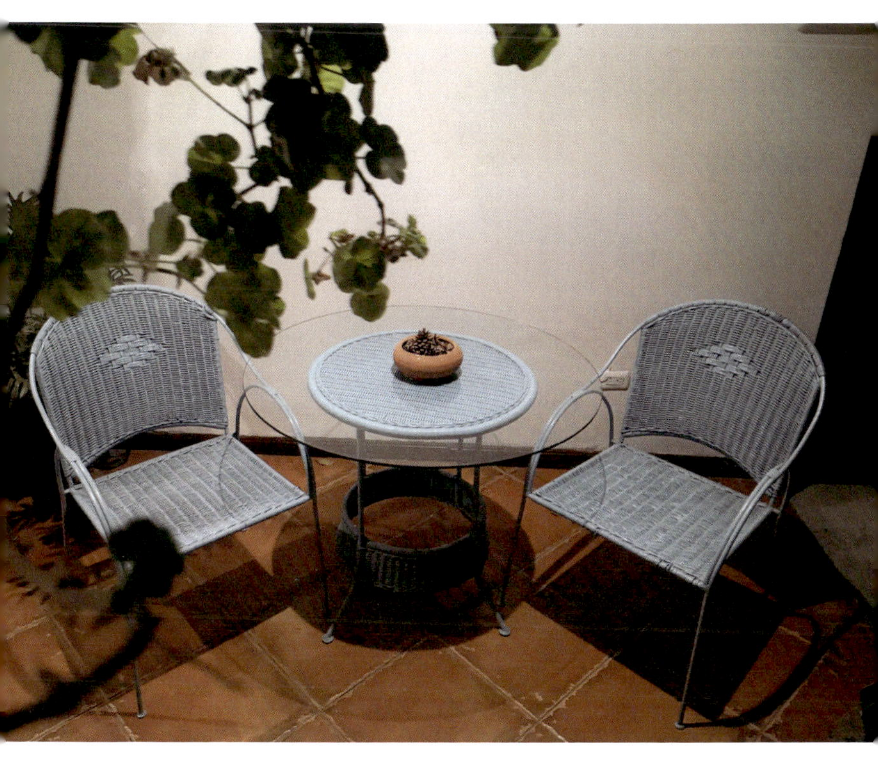

Lake of Memories

Nery Martinez Jr.

How often the nice things
go unappreciated,
misunderstood,

unreciprocated.

I miss the times
when things were less
complicated,

but what I really mean,
what really goes unsaid,
it's the missed opportunities that remind me
this is the time,
this is today,
this is it and not
what would've been.

A more grateful heart,
a more peaceful mind,
it's the realization I can't lose this time,
again.

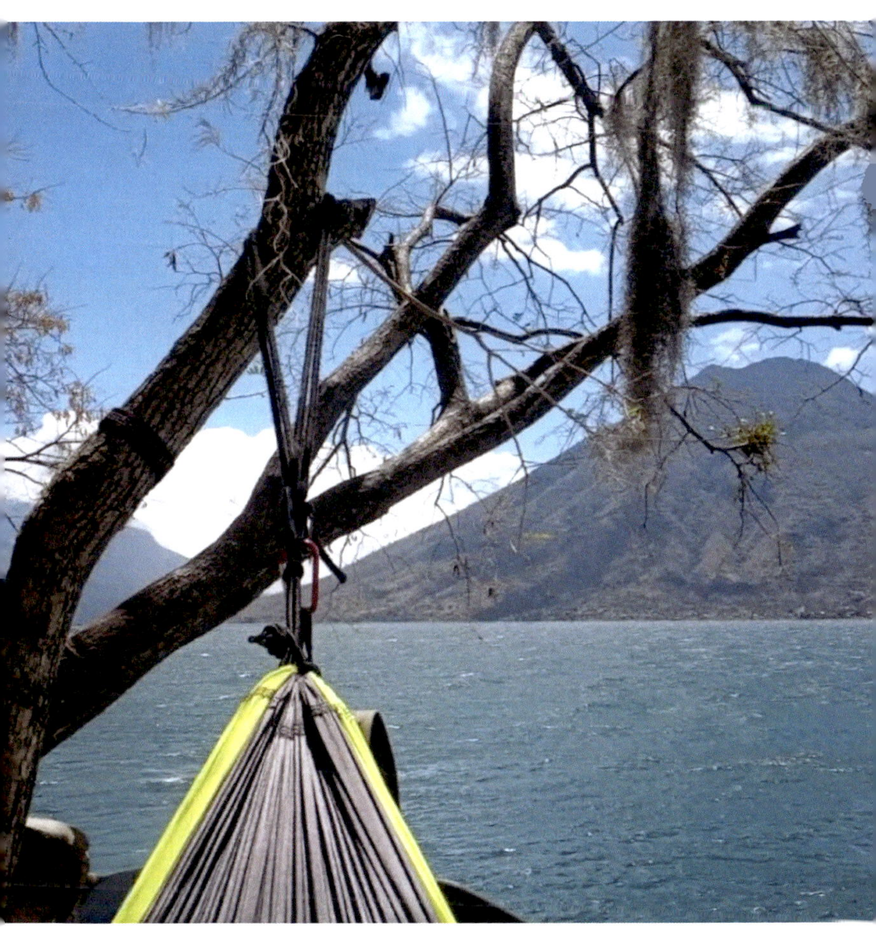

Weeks Go By

Gabriela Martinez

My weeks turn to days, and the days turn to hours,
almost like the flowers you gifted me that helped uplift me
when I needed it most.
My hours turn into minutes that turn into seconds,
I'm never spared for I am prepared,
the best is yet to come.
So far it is nearby.
It is as if my weeks are only days and months are only weeks
flashing by.
I can feel myself crashing, though I am dancing.
I know in the near future that will be full of adventure,
I'd capture each memory from each venture.

Mi Gente

Gabriela Martinez

When visiting Mexico, Mi Gente
I smell the leña, the burnt wood we used to cook our dinners with
In the distance I hear música playing from a car nearby while my
    family sings along, todos cantando.
Once the food is done cooking, the flavor that hits my tongue is
    everlasting, el sabor nunca se acaba.
The sun is setting, oh how there's no better view than from a
    mountain top, el monte.
The warmth of the fire used while cooking hits you like brownies
    fresh out of the oven baked.
Mexico feels the most relaxing when the days are spent like these,
    I always visit every chance I can.

Sugar From the Sea

Julie Rico

Seems like yesterday
when you looked up at me
through your Zorro's mask.

Remember how we trekked the city
my hand held tightly to your leash
with a quick gait to our feet.

We walked past the
The morass of humanity.
Good and bad,
strong and weak,
rich and poor.

You my little Biggy spreading to all
a little joy as you pranced.
A wide smile always glued to your face.

Years have passed since those days,
when we set out on our journeys exploring
downtown L.A. walking proudly
even as the hot, gray concrete
scorched our feet
and the black, sticky asphalt roads melted
in front of us.

Sometimes we even touched the ocean.
It's salty essence covering your coat like sugar
from the sea.

Once we traveled to Washington D.C.
We found a grassy path to tread,
you rolled in the cool greenness that
laid before us like an endless carpet.
I never saw you so happy.

Do you remember Biggy the dirt path at the State Park?
It was our favorite place of respite.

I caught a glimpse of you today, Biggy,
soaring through the sky with a heart in your paws.
You were sending me love and comfort,
A reminder of how magical you always were.
Remember when I tried to spank you?
You jumped up to hug and kiss me
And I realized what pure love was.
You taught me a lesson in Buddhist
Teachings–to never hurt a living thing.
That moment changed me forever.

As I was hit so often growing up it seemed
normal to spank dogs and kids.
But it is not.

Life should be this way with your heart always in mine
–without abuse.

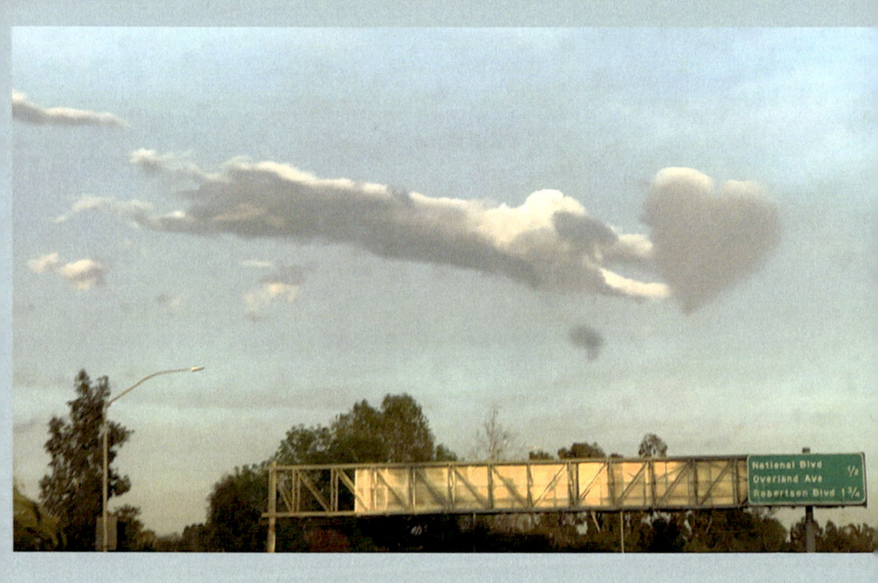
National Blvd 1/2
Overland Ave
Robertson Blvd 1 3/4

Love is in The Smoke

Julie Rico

This Buddhist temple is my rock in the storm

Mostly day to day I thrash around,
then feel the pain

I live in a giant turbulent sea
of a life I cannot tame
I throw a line around this place of quietude

I snatch it tight then beg, please
keep me from a loveless world

Ommm
Ommm
Ommm

Let us begin our meditation
Our minds are one
We can heal the world
We can heal ourselves
We can give hope for
those that need it

Ommm
Ommm
Ommm

Breathe the fog of sandalwood incense
It carries the power of the monks' thoughts

Love is in the smoke
it sneaks into the cracks,
into the crevices,
into your pain

for those who want to be on a plane of love with us
There is room for you

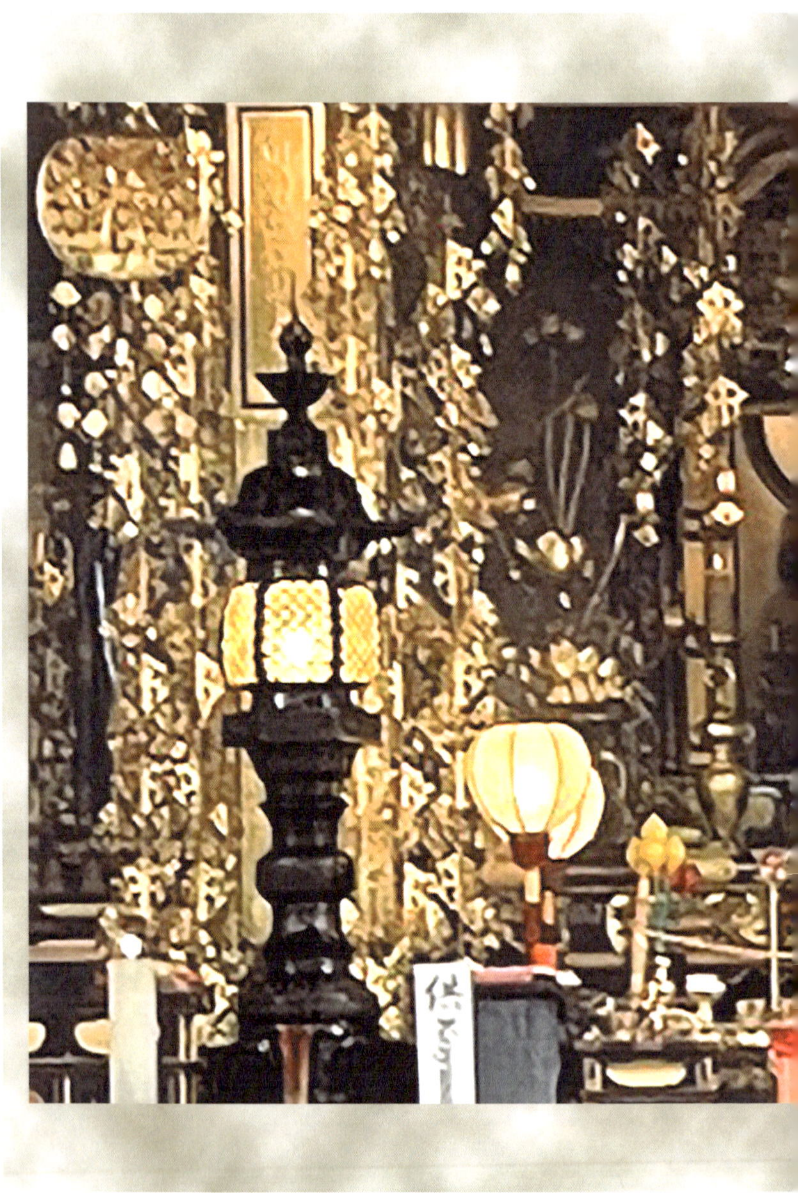

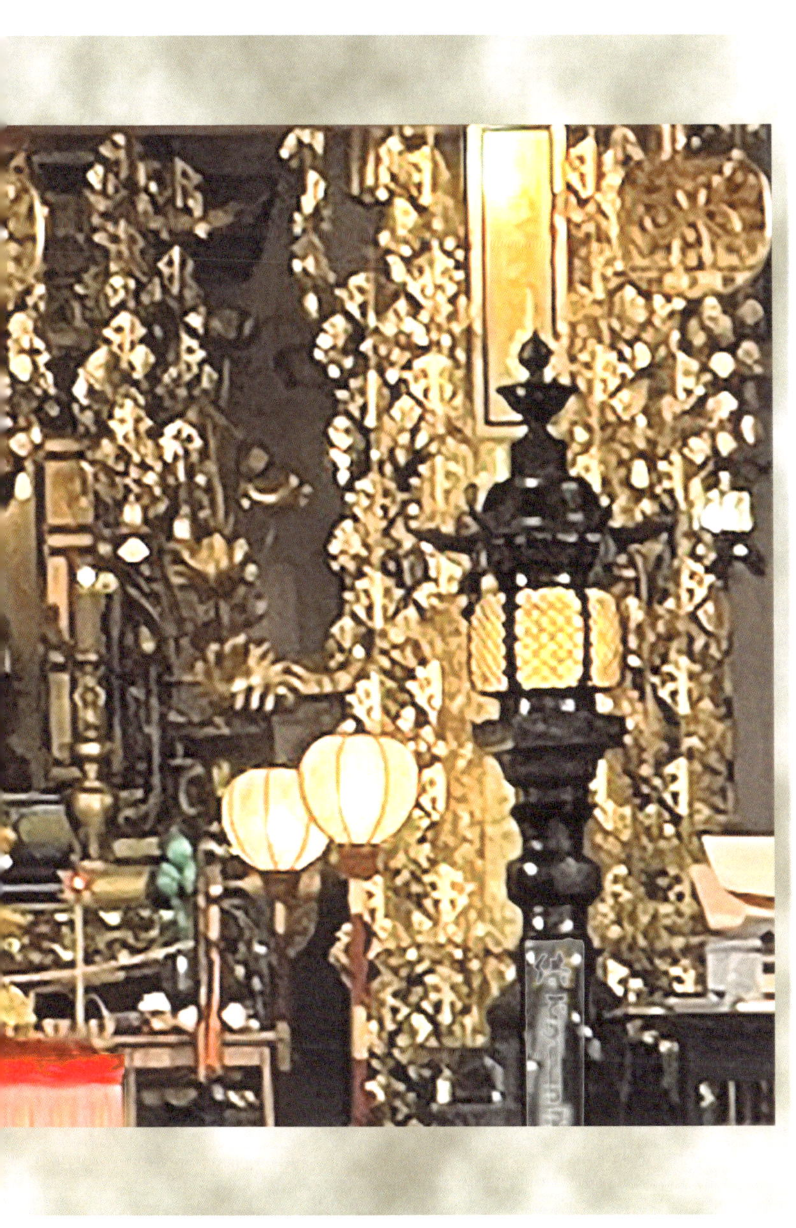

Treasures Lost in the Sand

Julie Rico

Look at their
their heads in the sand
Their secret language
execute actions to shame her

They care little for the
treasures of her mind

Lost in shame
There is no escape
Except inside her soul

Look at them as they kick
her feelings into a chasm

The fissure reaches deep
into the core of the earth
–all her ideas, her thoughts,
And her wishes

Buried there
Lie there
Die there

Quietly they impale her into a life
of servitude, obedience
and agonizing denial

Every day another woman's mind
is thrown into the chasm

As women's treasures wait
to be uncovered
the world
lies in a state of unbalance

Uncover the women's treasure
Then the world will flourish
beyond any man's imagination

In the garden women
were not touched by
the minds of primitive men

Women were revered
as the mirrors of the earth
Gaia pulsed with healing energy
The earth did thrive

Gaia
gave birth to the animals,
to the insects
to the plants to the people,
to the birds
and to all of the domestic animals, we call friends

It was Gaia a woman who
carried it all on her strong back

Gaia is woman

Women give everything to
make this earth
your world beautiful

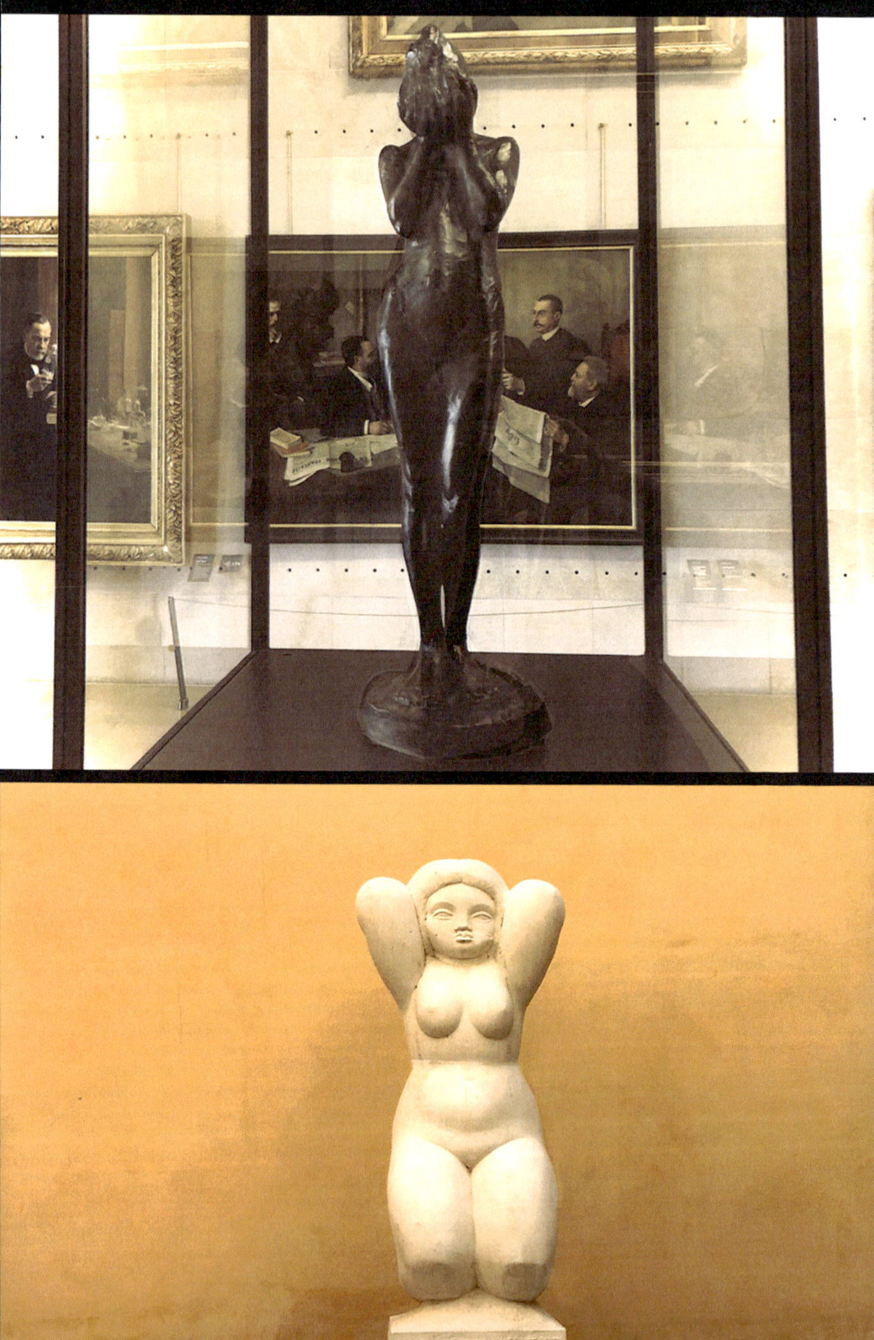

Whipping in the Wind

Julie Rico

Today as in millennia

We see the blue
We see the yellow
We see the green
The red the white

Whipping in the wind

The flags embody
our sacrifices for
The blood of Kings

Whipping in the wind

The dreams of our brothers

Whipping in the wind

and their souls left on
the battlefield as chattel

Whipping in the wind

The flags carry
The pain
the loss of
My friends
My family
Of my AMORES

Whipping in the wind

Each flag no matter where it's

from smells of greed

Whipping in the wind

Each flag brings sadness

I see
Loss
Dead Children
Maimed Children

I see a world
with no love, no hope

Our worlds reek of death

I know the powerful carry their flag as a shield

It helps ease their memory
It helps them to deny
It helps them to exploit

As they reap the rewards
From the demise of good people

There is little sadness
from the men
who profit
from behind the flags

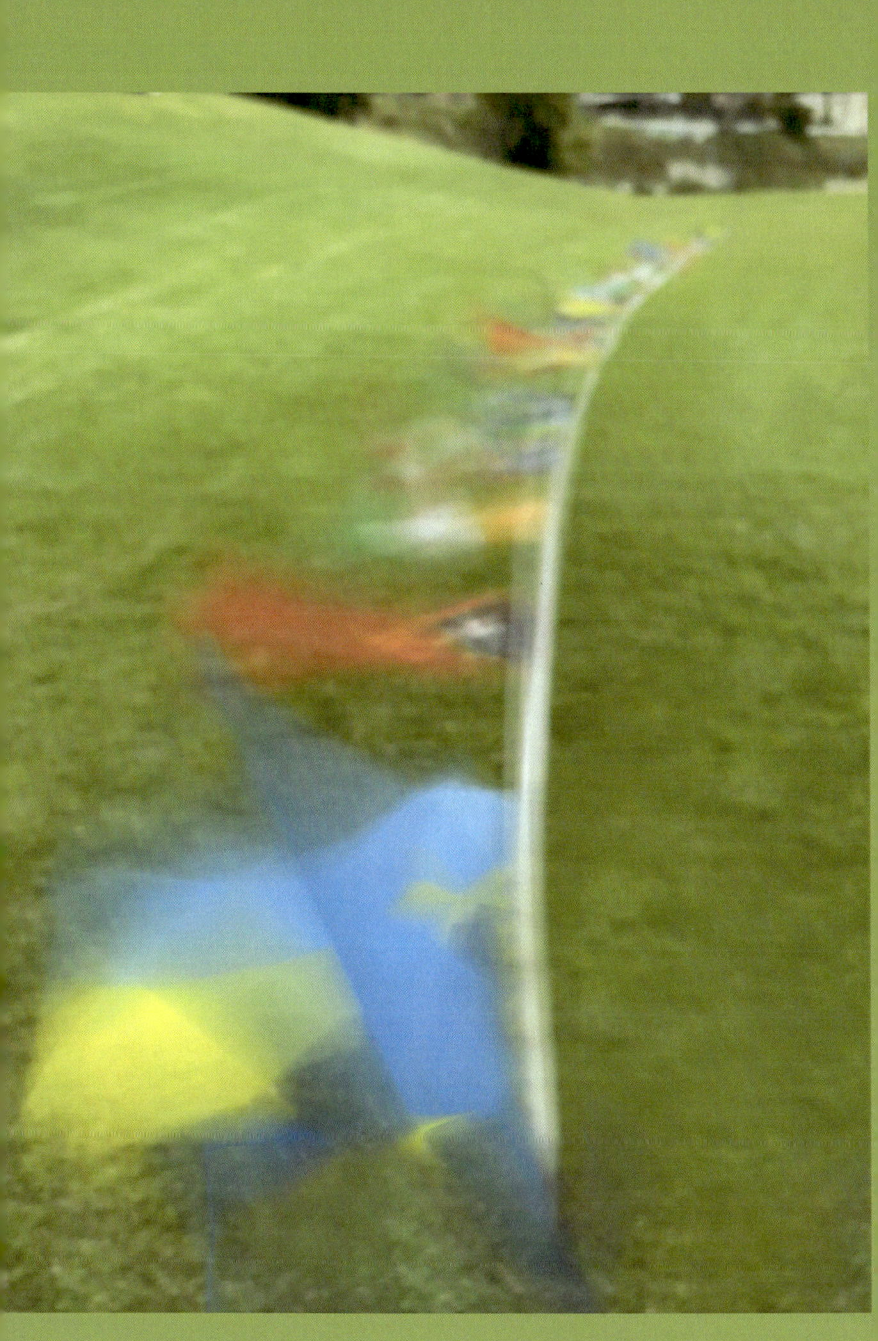

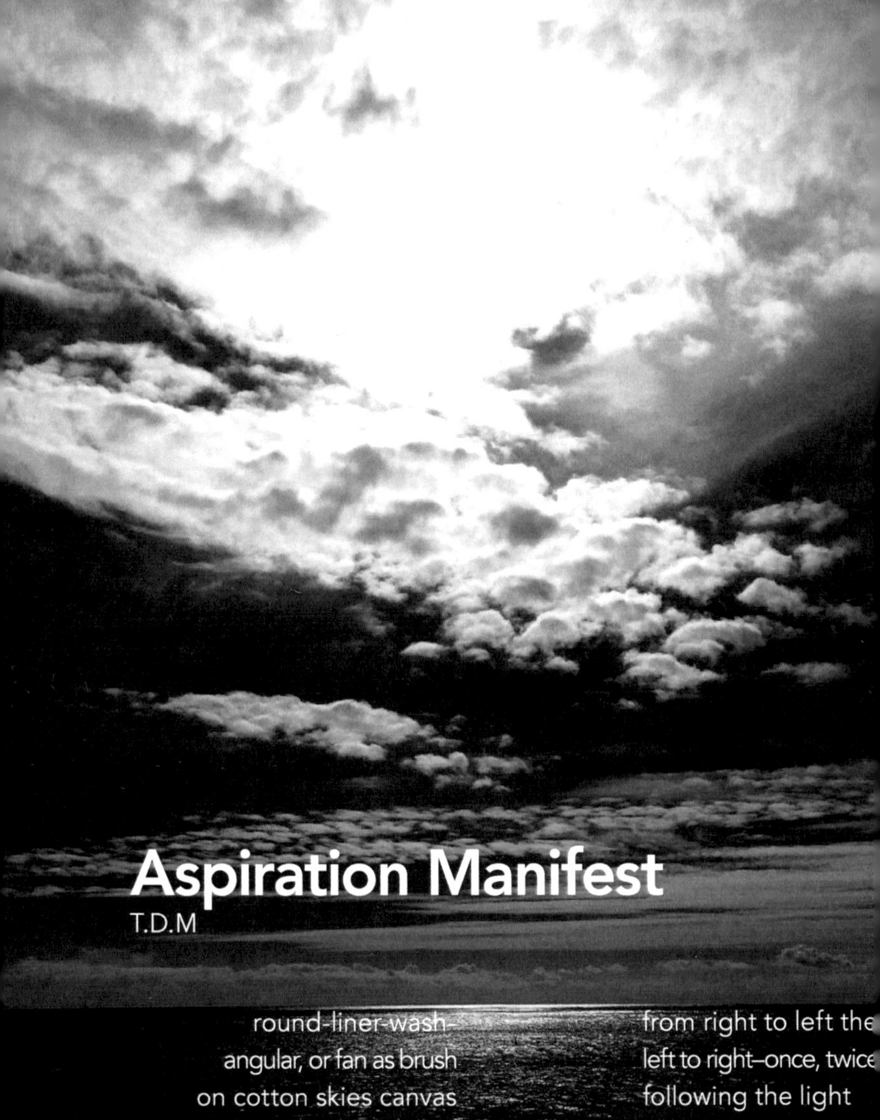

Aspiration Manifest

T.D.M

round-liner-wash-
angular, or fan as brush
on cotton skies canvas

electrifying
water wave in heaven's light
sea-clouds rolling by

from right to left the
left to right–once, twice
following the light

in zig-zag motions
one final destinatio
a line horizon

Offbeat

T.D.M.

When going for a stroll, one might avoid going during a cold silence. A cold that reigns over all that is living and elicits fear–tree branches silently shivering, leaves miming, no flowers dancing, or animals parading. Especially, don't stroll, while in cold silence, heading down a path uncharted; wearing flip flops flopping ready to retire. The sounds of pit pat, pit pats, pit patting echo as cheap rubber meets gravel and sand. Why couldn't I have worn proper sneakers instead? That cold silence–uncharted path–flip flops flopping–makes me wish I was still in bed.

Oh!

Civilization ahead. Typically for me, there isn't anything wrong being in nature's majesty; and seeing a familiar tar-laden road is a thing of glory. One step, two step, three–I'll continue following the clouds, in dewdrop ballet, floating above the two faint white lines ahead; adorned with trees on both sides. Wet feet now cramping–while flip flops flopping, down an uncharted path, in cold silence.

Euphoria!

Finally, a path lit for me in glorious oranges and ambers–cramping feigning–flip flops stopping–cold silence warming–life now moving–a carnival of sound. Hills rolling in waves, like a calm ocean, quietly buoying a sunrise's glory; lifting cloudy grays. Morning's beauty beholden me! So, I am taking back what I said–it's better to go for that stroll during cold silence instead.

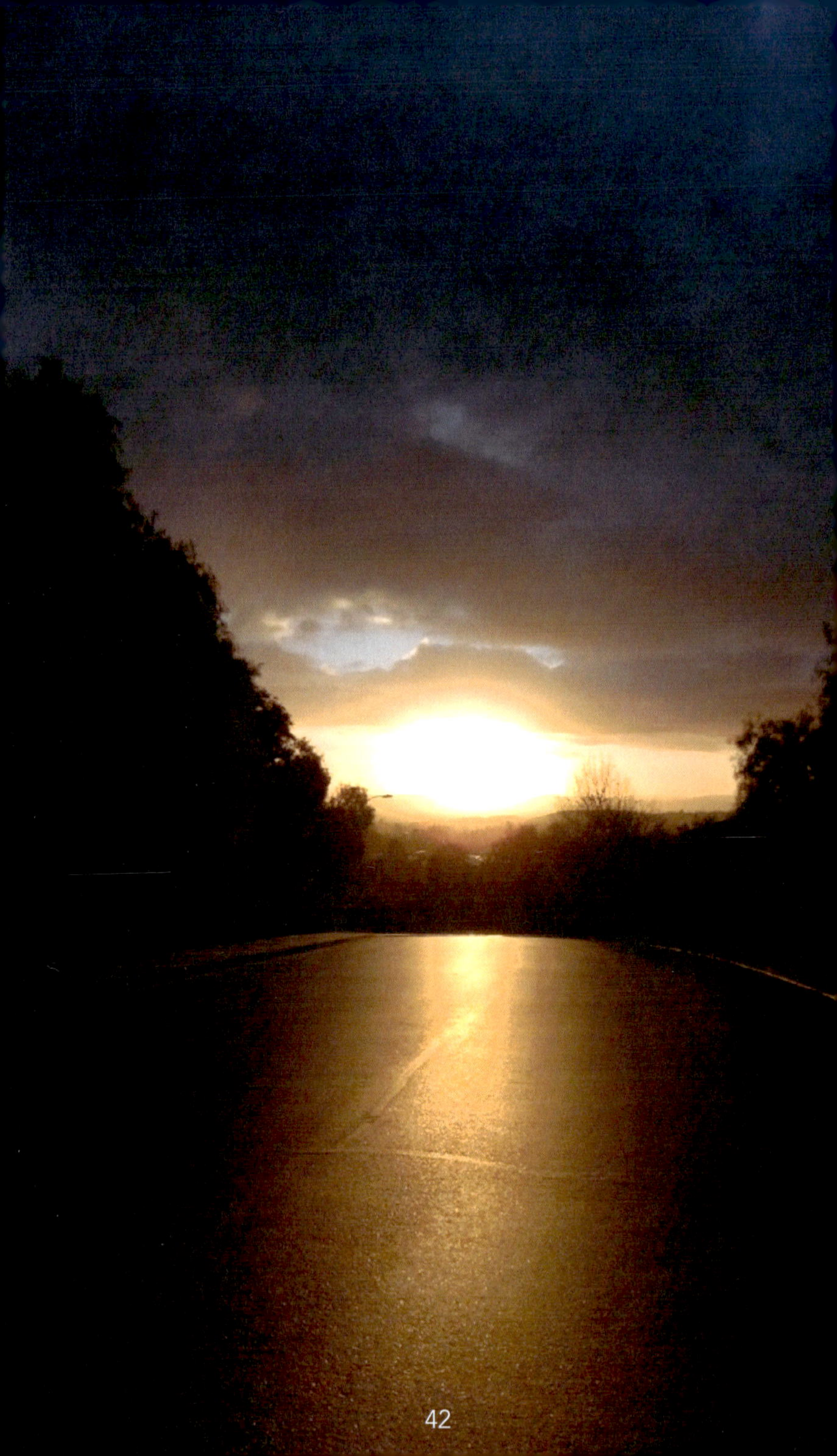

Six and Sky

T.D.M

The six raven's flyby so serene during sunset
of angular formation their bodice
rigid, sable, in aerodynamic origami

soaring pre-night's atmosphere
the six fly mid-velocity with a tailwind
their feathers' glossy reflections

seen above a city valley horizoned
readying slumber starting half midnight
jet setting introspection the six fly carrying

wisdom, philosophy the six emanate
or maybe dewdrops of intuition
with hope helping helpless sing

though the heading is unknown
let the six fly clear skies and
ample wind during winter's sunset

closing unto the first of spring
the one staggering might
head the six to where heart's sunlight sings

An Impossible City / An Unrivaled City

Marjan Modarres Sabzevari

This collection observes women from a different perspective, via the lens of a tourist's camera.

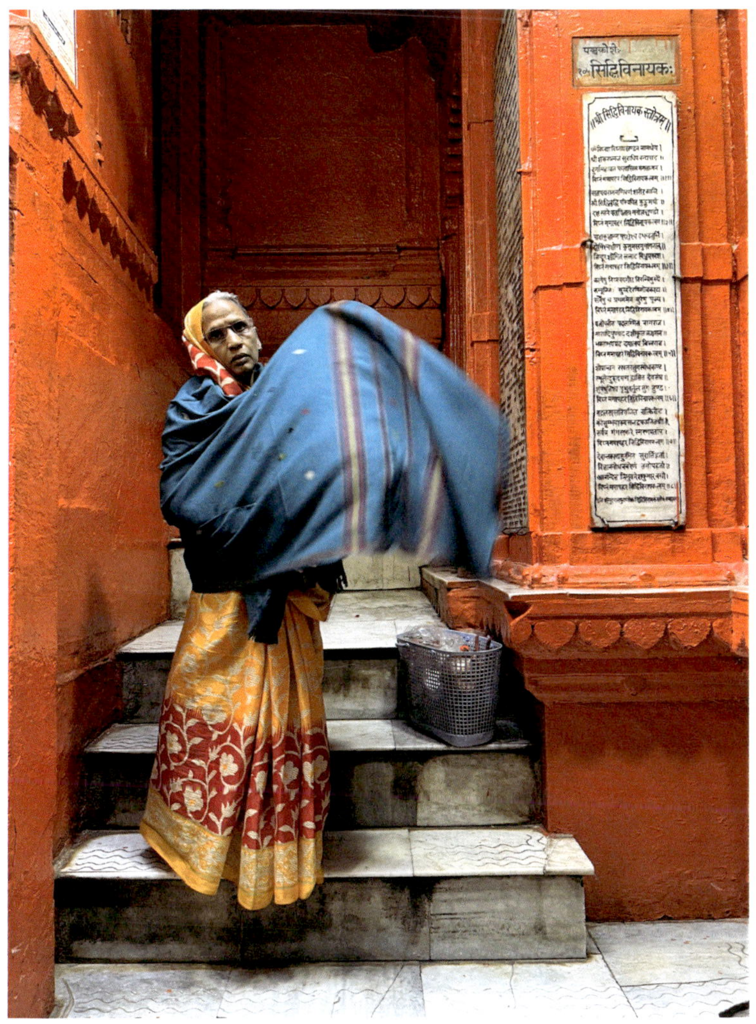

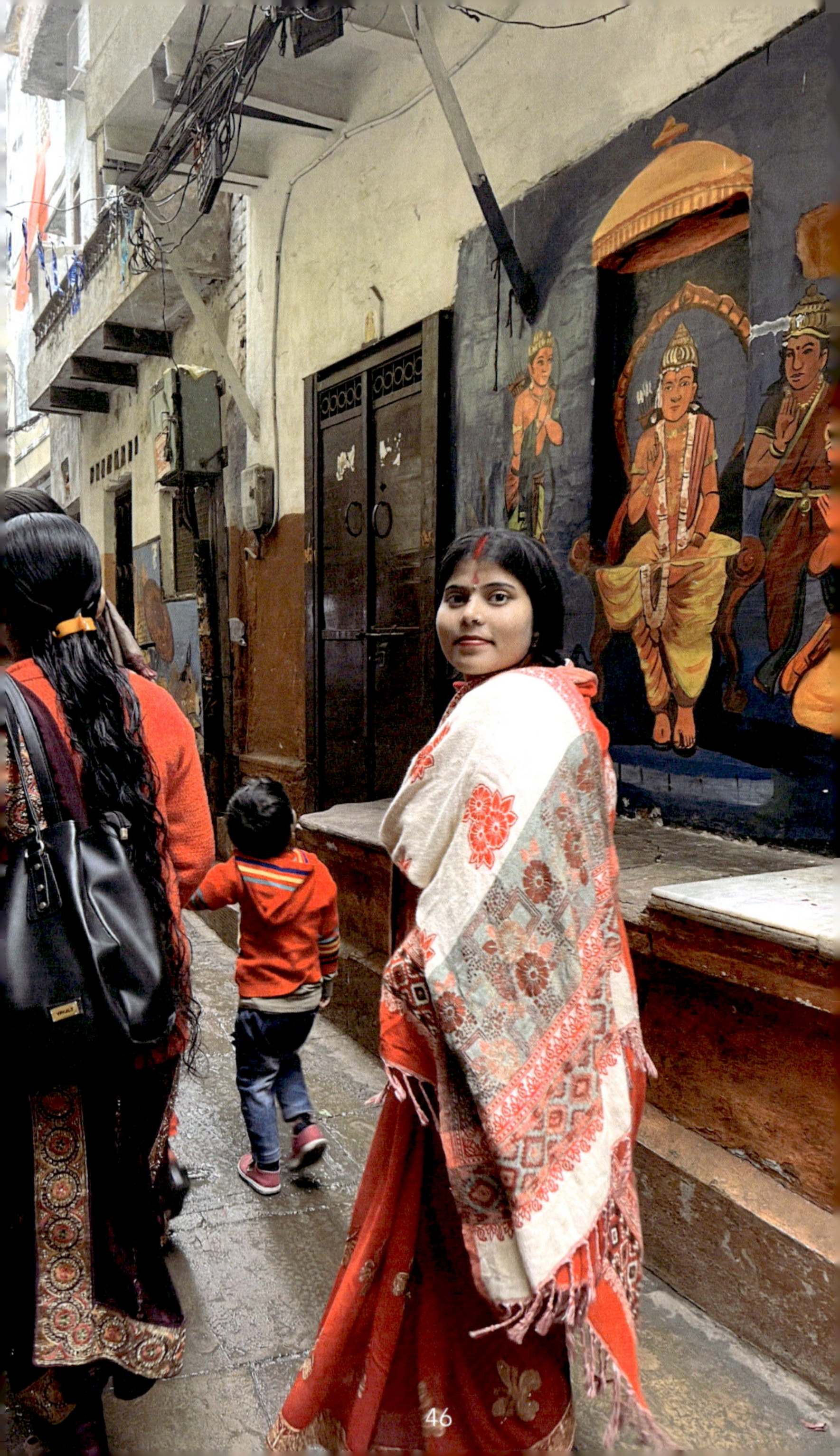

Lost You

Mojdeh Amini

Lost you
on the earth of
my childhood mind

found you
In the heart of sky

Now your eye
without blinking
touches
my feelings
my tenderness
my shadows
my darkness

when it comes
and goes like
Winds

A Mirror

Mojdeh Amini

a framed mirror
hanging on

a break wall painted
in half & half
creamy grey patches
in a narrow street

It's there for everyone
and everything,

resting last night with
lonely moon counting countless
stars

busy during the day counting
everyone, everything in
thousands
counting the shadows
of thousands lives

days after days
weeks after weeks

years after years
street and trees

buildings and windows
watching and observing

the busy life through the
eye of the mirror

with no filtering
neither zoning
even has many chance to shoot
but will be never the same

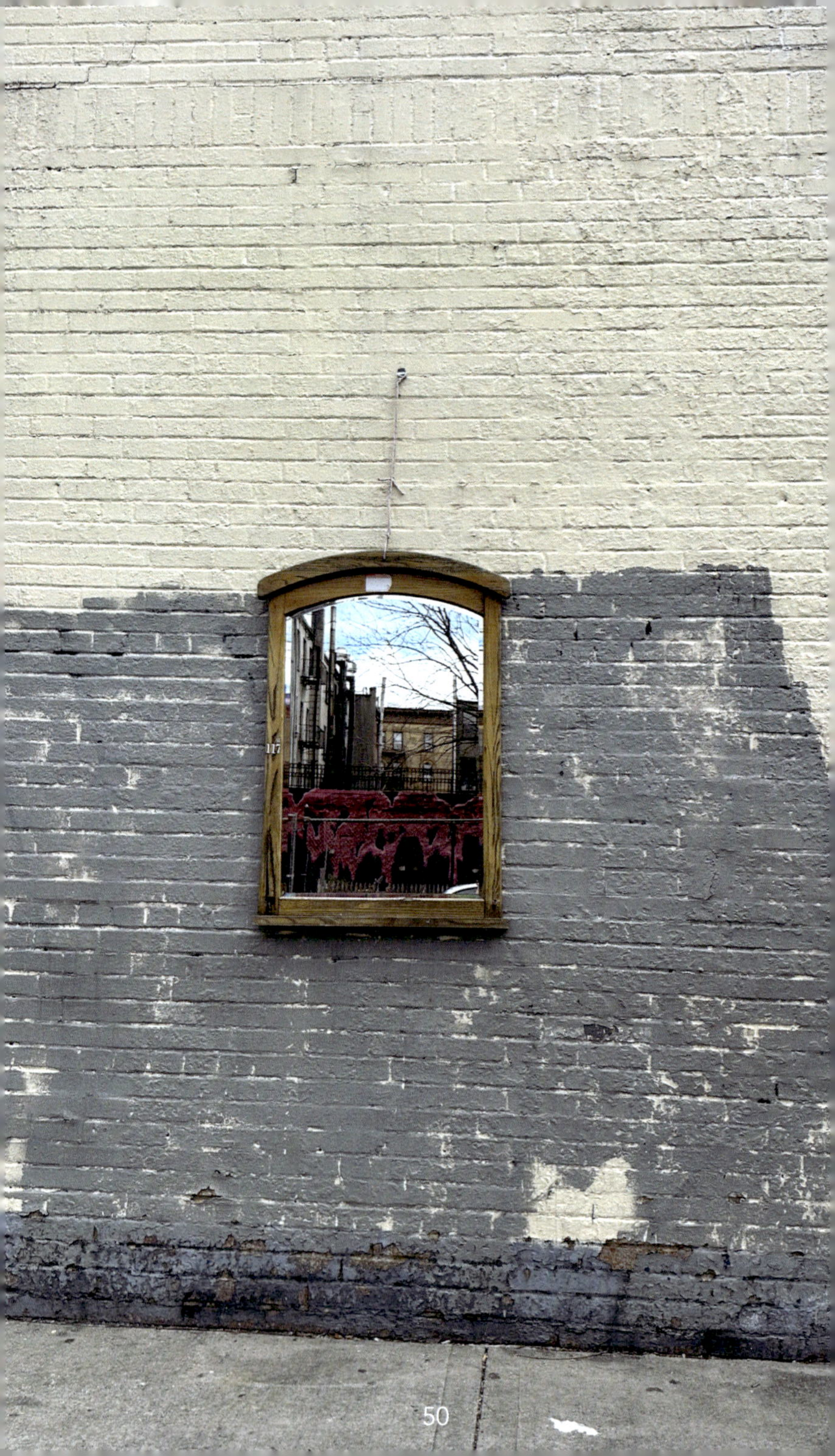
117

An Absolute

Mojdeh Amini

In an absolute
darkness of a
bright day
in a rainy day

In rush hours
rain hits the rusted rails
washes and leaves
many dust and dirts behind

At the
last stop
train turns
its mood

Calm to warrior
local to express
circle to diamond
green to red

Rushes to meet
the lights
at the end of
the tunnel

In speed of
faster than lights
leaves a head
to toe scar

a sky to earth scar
but to reach to touch
to feel and to stand the
darkness of the lights

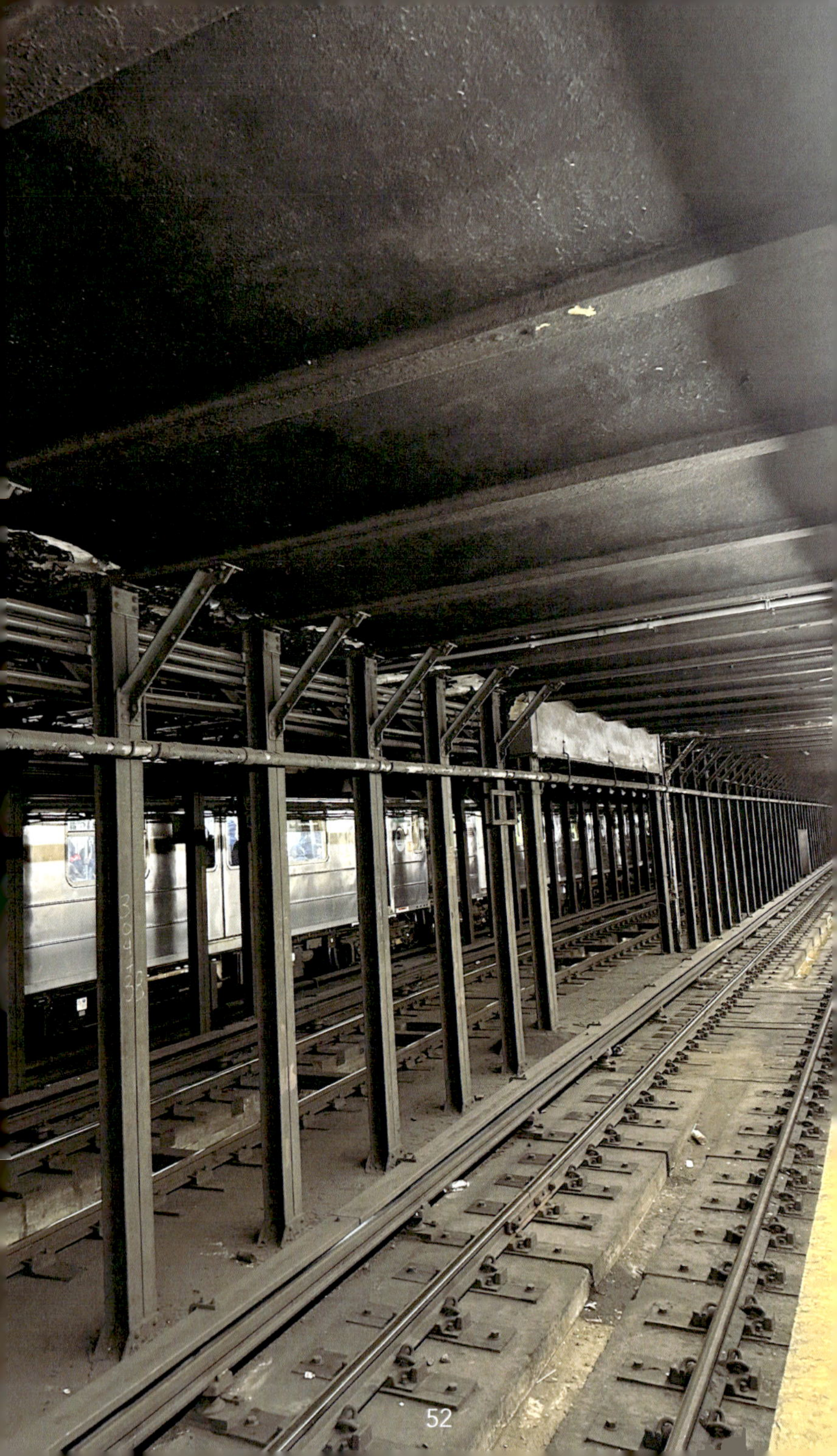

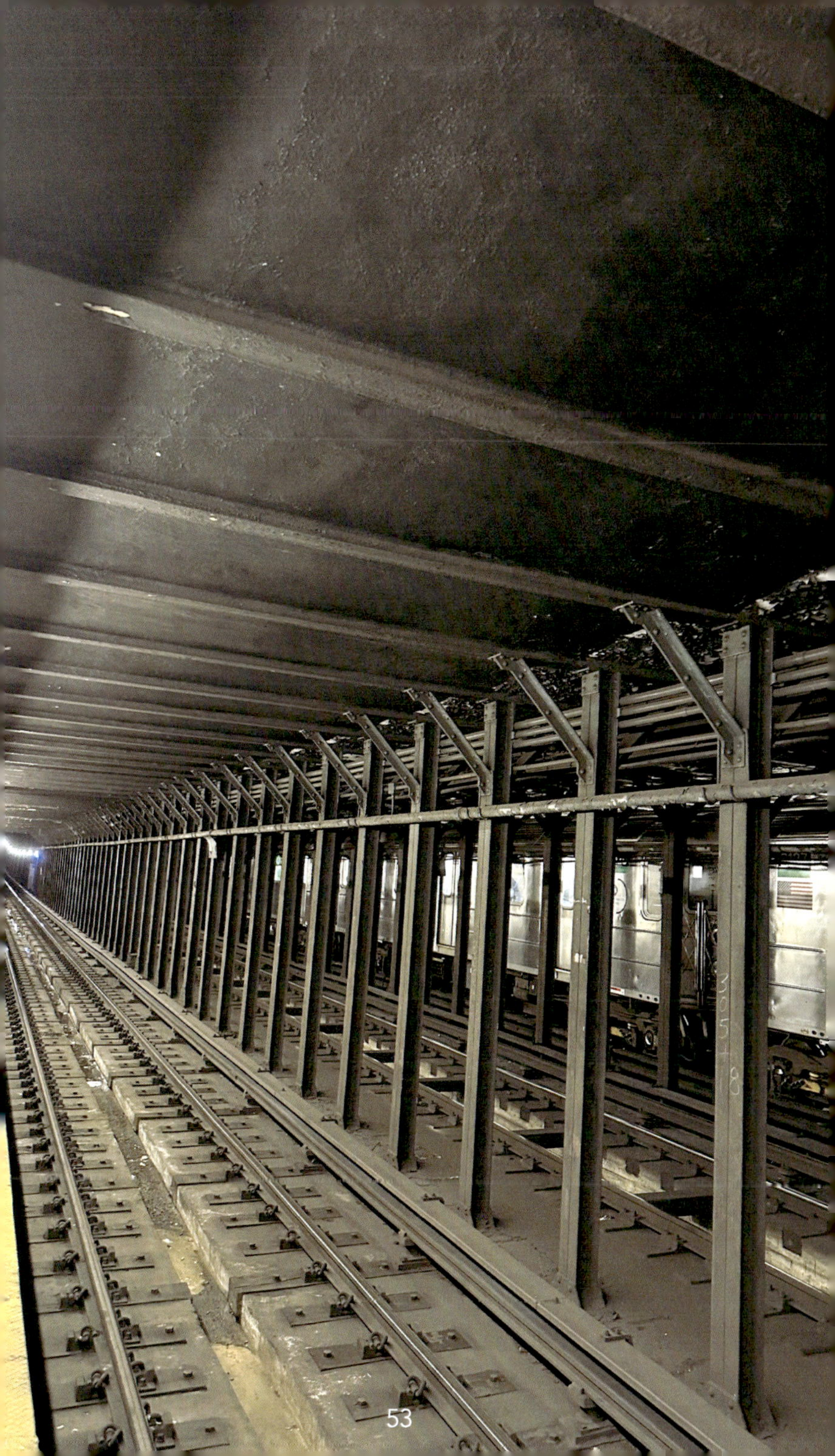

Who Knows (Stripped Down)

Mojdeh Amini

who knows
what the tree was thinking
when stripped down to
the earth to give
its nobility of soul to
the existence of the
winter

who knows
what the tree was thinking
when dropped down
its pulchritude leaves to
the ground to louden
beauty of the
winter

who knows
what the tree was thinking
when spreading
its branches of kindness to
the crescendo
the brutality of the
wheels

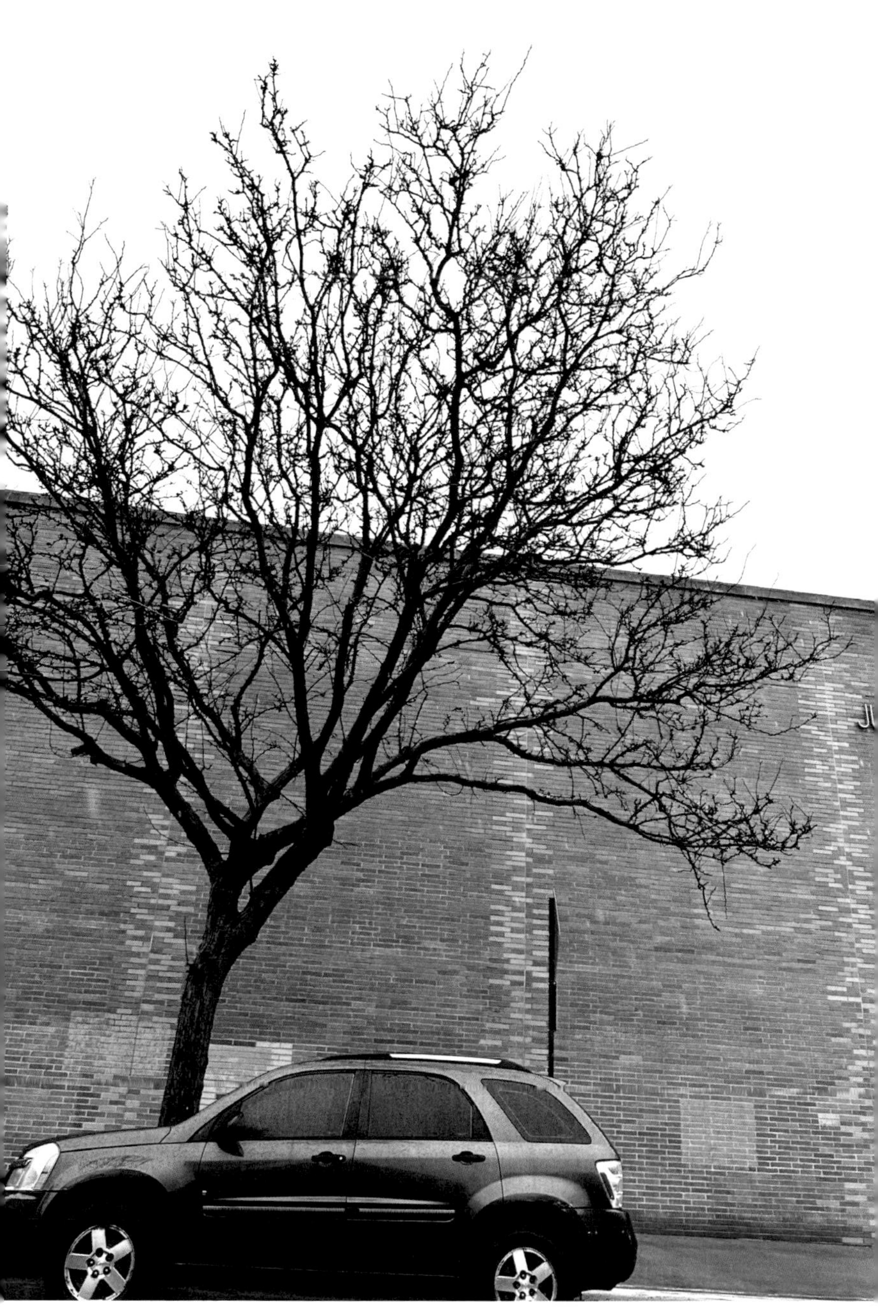

A Winter

Mojdeh Amini

A heavy
wild white winter

sprinkles silence
and slits ice

Into the air
settling on

the trees
Landing on

the ground
and water

a little
blackbird flies

flapping its wings
fluttering around

gives its wings
to the winds

to the clouds
breaks the silence

turns white clouds
into grey and black

Feeding the earth

but
the Mississippi River

remains calm
warm and watching

under the eyes
and cuddles of

the bridges
and icy water

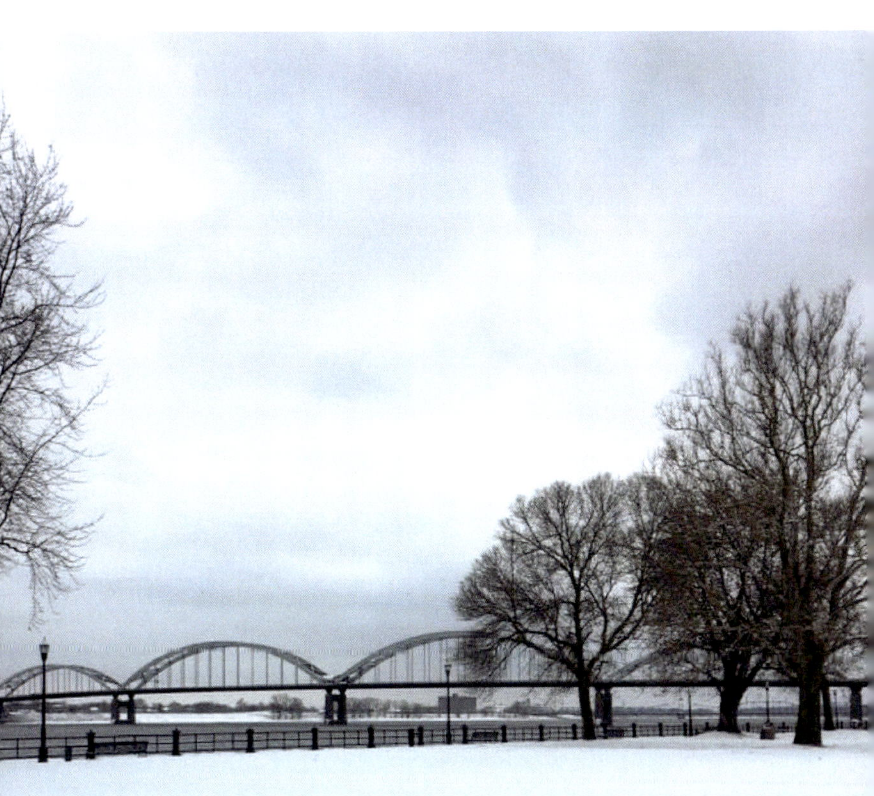

Made In Sky

Mojdeh Amini

linguist says
it's snowing,

it snows us into
its beauty

its silence
its fragile purity

Poem says,
clouds opened up

its magic spells
to the earth

searching
for dreams

stars,
showered off

the spells
over night

clouds opened up
its snowflacked

catching
the dreams

the sky closes up
its umbrellas

earth,
swells up in snow

flaked off

delight and laughters

showrooms
Joyfulness and happiness

to the sky and
to the earth

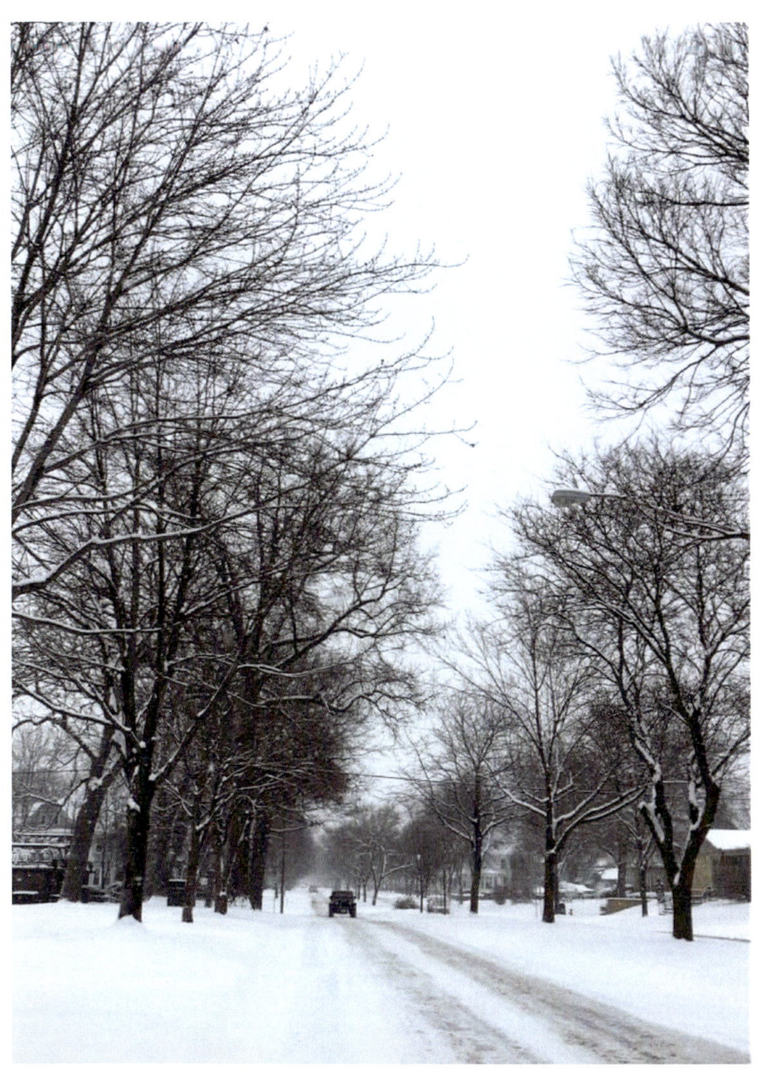

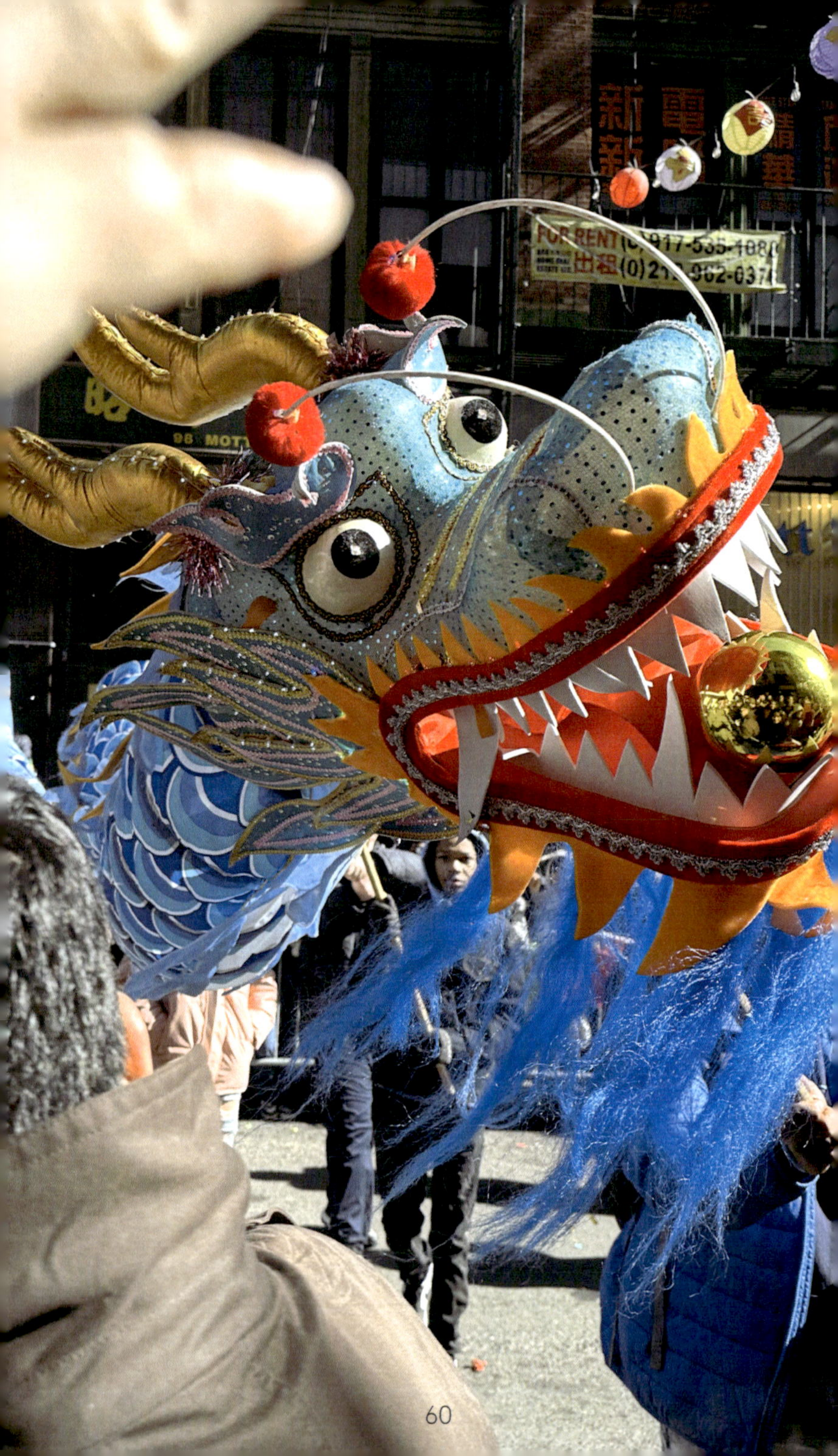
FOR RENT
出租

A Dragon

Mojdeh Amini

comes in colors
with not smokes, but
with wild wide smiles

comes in waves
with vigorous scary motions
with up and downing crowds

shows off its
golden generosity
locked in its sword teeth

with no tension and smells of fears
give it up to any but
bite any to take many

crowds don't care or scare
screaming loud with wide smile
with no doubt but comes to give

hands are trying to touch
to feel its magic gold without
reading its face and waves

as locked themselves
within the sword teeth
with ancient words of stars

A Girl

Mojdeh Amini

When it rains words
Spread my hair and
There is no need for any shades or branches

And when
Open my heart
There is no need for any doors and windows

Then when
Open my mind
There is no need for any codes and proses

Only poems are allowed

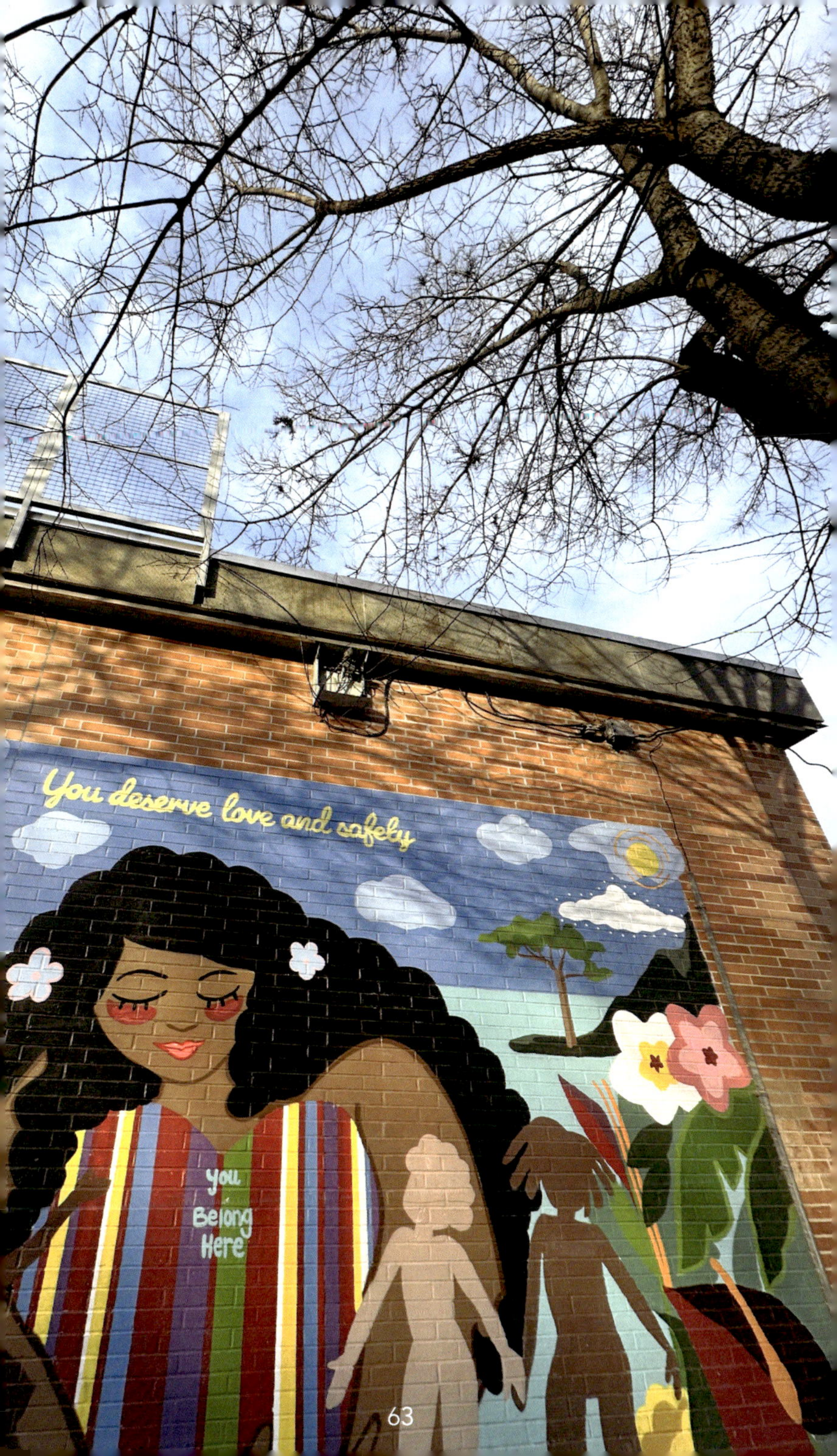
You deserve love and safety
You
Belong
Here

madreselva por piel

River

cuando tevengritan luces aullan porlanoche te tienenmiedo
        avertuspuntos vacíos

pero

sin   ti
  la vida   huye

si te pierde
me pierde

si te desapareces
  me disipo

si
esconder
es

morir   pues
  sí:
ocultar
de miedo
es matarme

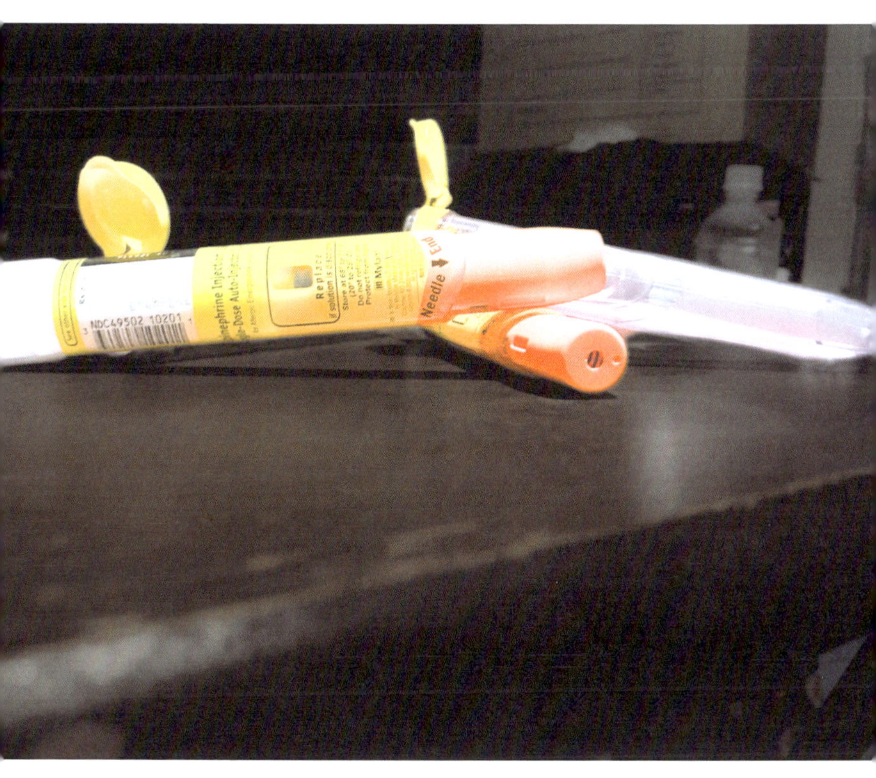
NDC49502 10201
Replace
Needle End

Motherjungle for Skin

River

when youtheyseetheycomeshout lights they howl thruthenight
    toseeyourpoints empty

but

without   you
  life   flees

if you get lost
i get lost

if you disappear
i dissipate

if
to hide
is

to die   then
  yes:
to obscure
from fear
is to kill me

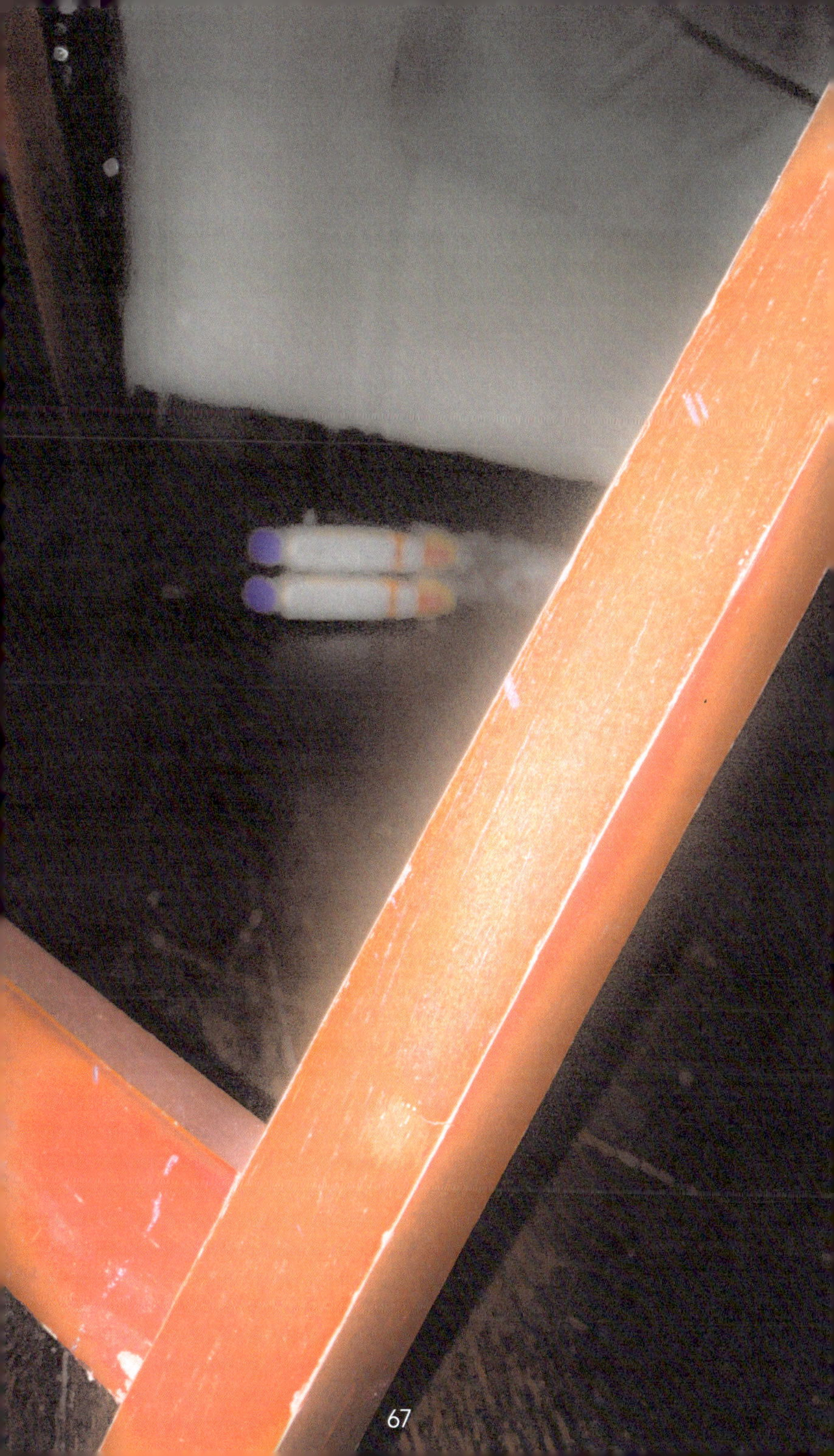

Balancing Act

Sanjuanita

You always stood there
Smile drawn across your face
Concocting ways to entertain,
To make me laugh.
You were younger,
"shorty" we called you.
Me, the big sister, proud and tall

You, climbing the tallest trees
Jumped off without fear
While I laughed at you.
Thinking I was the smart one.
Thinking I was the lucky one.

You kept secrets for me
The ones I thought would disown me,
Like the time I fought in school,
Like the time I kissed a boy,
Like the time I cussed in church,
You really saved me!
Poor you endured my bossiness
Making you clean my room
And doing the dishes for me.
Getting whatever I wanted
Even if it meant what you had.
All was just to please me.
Just to "measure up"
You knew what would happen
If you didn't.

Time elapsed... some things changed.

Bossiness is no more!
Keeping secrets is no more!

Laughter is no more!
Shorty is no more!

For time has passed.

There's you and a new me.
I see you, my brother.
The truth in your eyes
Was the balance I sought
In this life space.

Keep my balance, brother.
For I will keep yours, too.

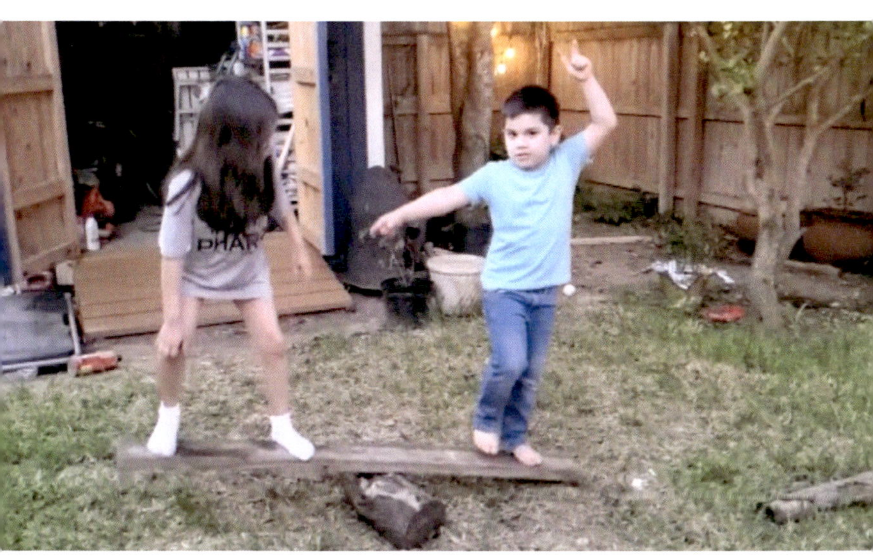

Before I Go And to Lengthen the Time

Sanjuanita

I must take the "road not taken"
And make new footprints.
I must revisit the old album
And reminisce once again.
I must see the northern lights
And relish this day.
I must go parachuting
And let myself go.
I must climb a mountain
And shout for joy.
I must forgive my enemies
And lighten my heart.
I must plant a tree
And add some flowers.
I must milk a cow
And feed the chickens.

I must stomp on puddles
And run without care.

I must take the long way home
And drive the winding road.
I must drink tequila shots
And savor it with salt.
I must light a campfire
To welcome the night.
I must complete a family tree
And celebrate my ancestors.
I must look for roses
Where there are thorns.
I must sew a dress

And wear it in summer.
I must paint sunsets
And call it a name.
I must draw sunrises
And pray for a sign.
I must sleep under the stars
And count them one by one.
I must fly a kite
And let it go high.
I must volunteer again
And live a full life.

Before I go,
And to lengthen the time.

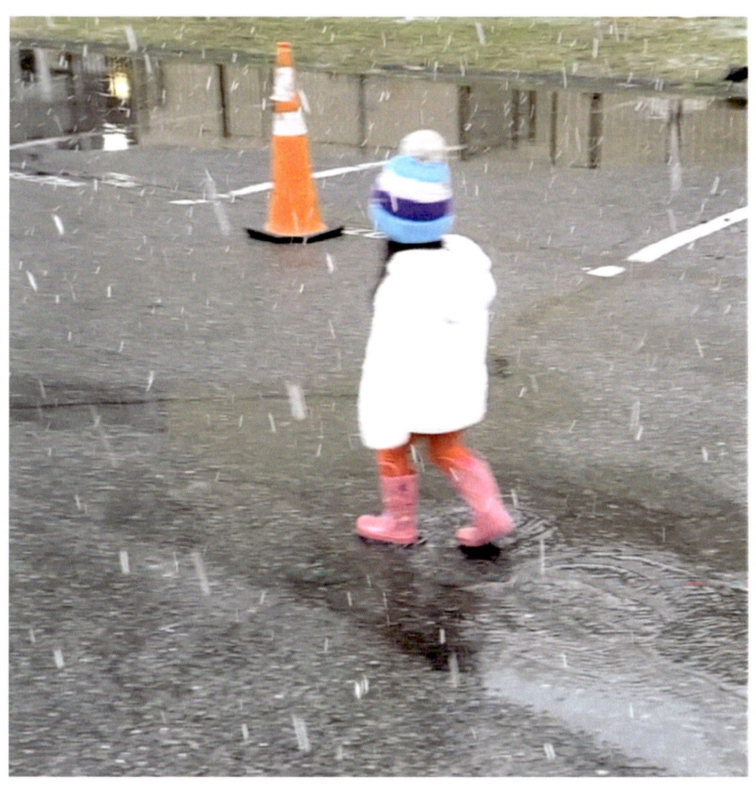

Twisted Fate

Sanjuanita

Too long a scrutiny.
A lengthy steady gaze
Hurtful utterances

At times stepped on
Trampled for
being different.

A dreaded fear
Resisting, revolting
Trying to make it alive.

It is different, unique
But no one sees it,
Only you.

Mixture of colors: green, yellow, brown, orange, red.
Depicting an array of emotions.

Anger, joy,
frustration, success,
Sadness, joy,
Weakness, endurance,

Still it Embarks
In Adventures
Even without a rudder,

It feels
Collected
Privileged
And accepted at times.

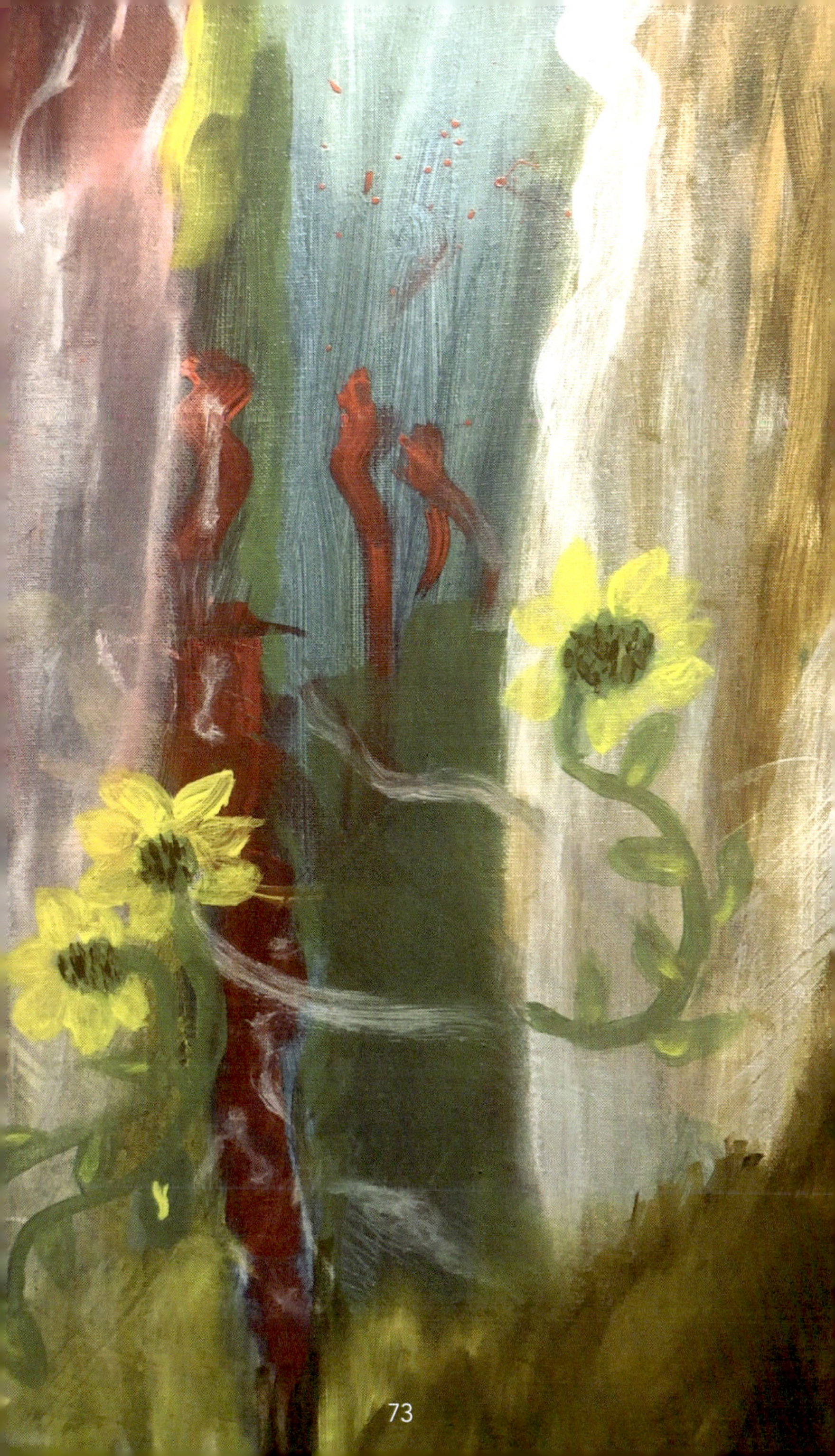

Good

Sanjuanita

No matter what surrounds you,
Give of yourself without a doubt.

In any tough dark space
Shine your light.

In the midst of turmoil,
Lend a hand.

In times of hatred,
Sing a song of love.

In the middle of deserts,
Encourage the weary.

In the most selfless way
Feed the hungry.

In the most generous way,
Clothe the needy.

In the most unselfish way,
Fill the world with love.

In the most loving way,
be the light In the darkness.

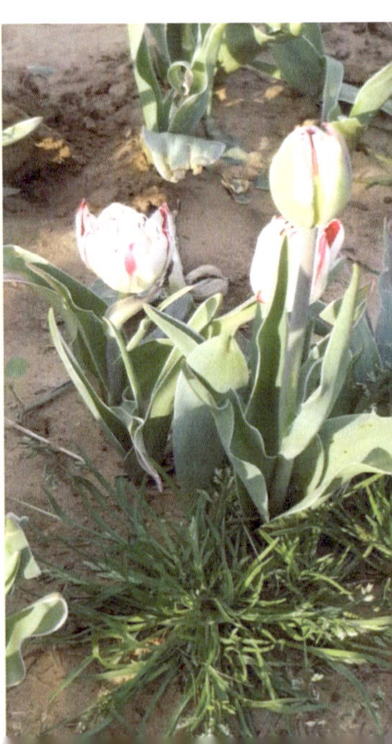

Evil

Sanjuanita

The forbidden fruit
was taken.
With it, the wicked plan
was constructed.
Infamous characters
and their cursed thoughts
mangled and altered the plan.
The vicious cycle of sin,
selfishness, pride, and justice
were awakened...
The ungodly plans
now reign.
Now Evil has many faces.
Which we may not know.

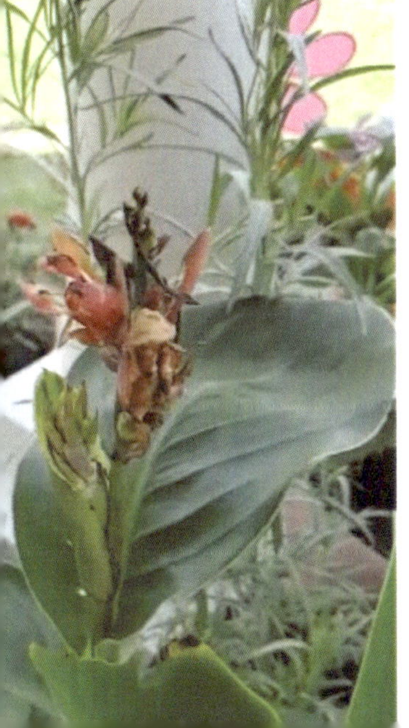

Words Untold

Sanjuanita

Plans, dreams
Of places to go
Words untold
Trapped in oblivion
In the trenches
Where we said we'd fight.
No empire to build
Like we once said
Of layers upon layers
Of promises
Of stories
Of memories
We said we could
Gone is the march
Towards the horizon
Parallel lines
Is what we have
And the words
The worlds
The stories
Will never be known.

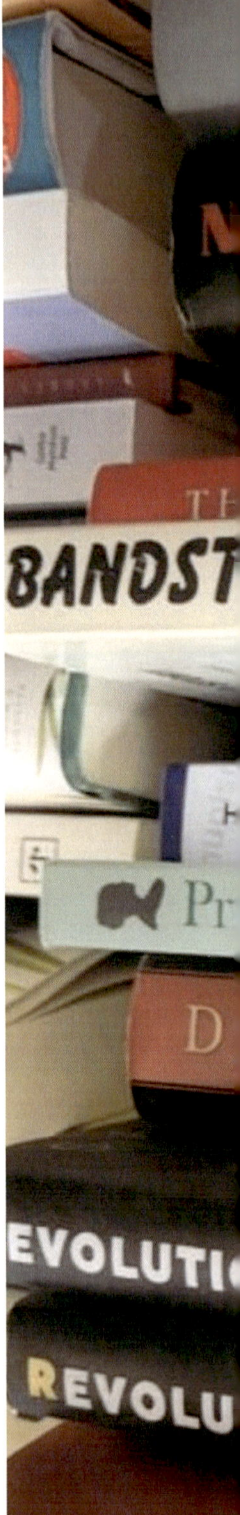

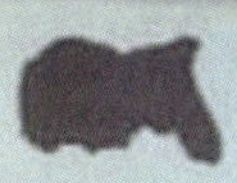

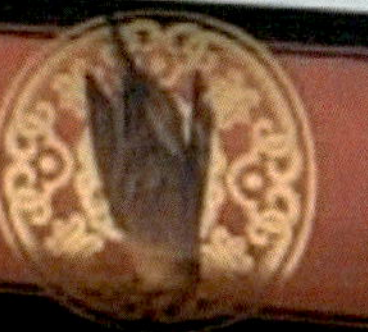

JERA ESCAPE ARTIST
Dreamland
ADVENTURES IN THE STRANGE SCIENCE OF SLEEP
DAVID
WORDS
TIM GLYNNE-JONES
, THE UNTOLD STORY
STANLEY J. B
AS TOLD TO
JOHN PRITCHAR
The Inner Life
INNER LAND
THE LANGUAGE OF LIBERTY
Prejudice & Puzzles
RICHARD GALLAND
IPLINE
PACO AHLGR
F THE SOUL
SEANE CORN
OF THE SOUL

No Death Till Do Us Part

Sanjuanita

It's like nothing occurred.
          To wither and fall
What once became a dream
Gigantic dreams of forever
To cherish and hold
Till death do us part
In illness and in health

          Wasn't it a promise?

It's like nothing occurred
Like a not happily ever after
Your not very typical ending
Not a fairy tale,
No cinderella
No Snow White.
No prince to awake me.

A house with many windows.
Some facing the sun.
With a light coming through
          Some facing dark
With images of uncertainty

A future wraparound porch
That may strangle what
          Was the plan
          To spend time sipping coffee
With the many sunsets
          That now will never be.
          That will never be.

Lights flickered off
Dry creaking sounds

Wind seeping through
Limbs shamelessly
          Opening the roof
As if saying, "This is mine, leave!"
Not mine anymore
Not mine forever
No death here
Till do us part.

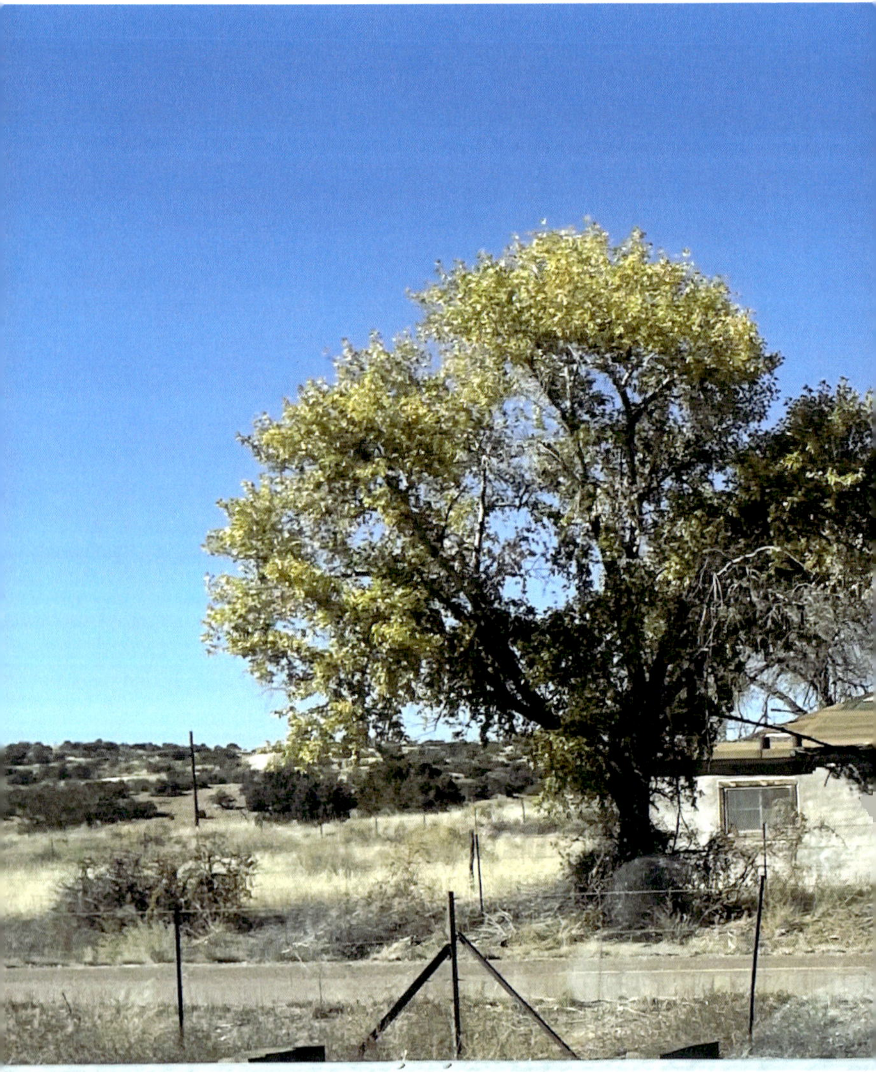

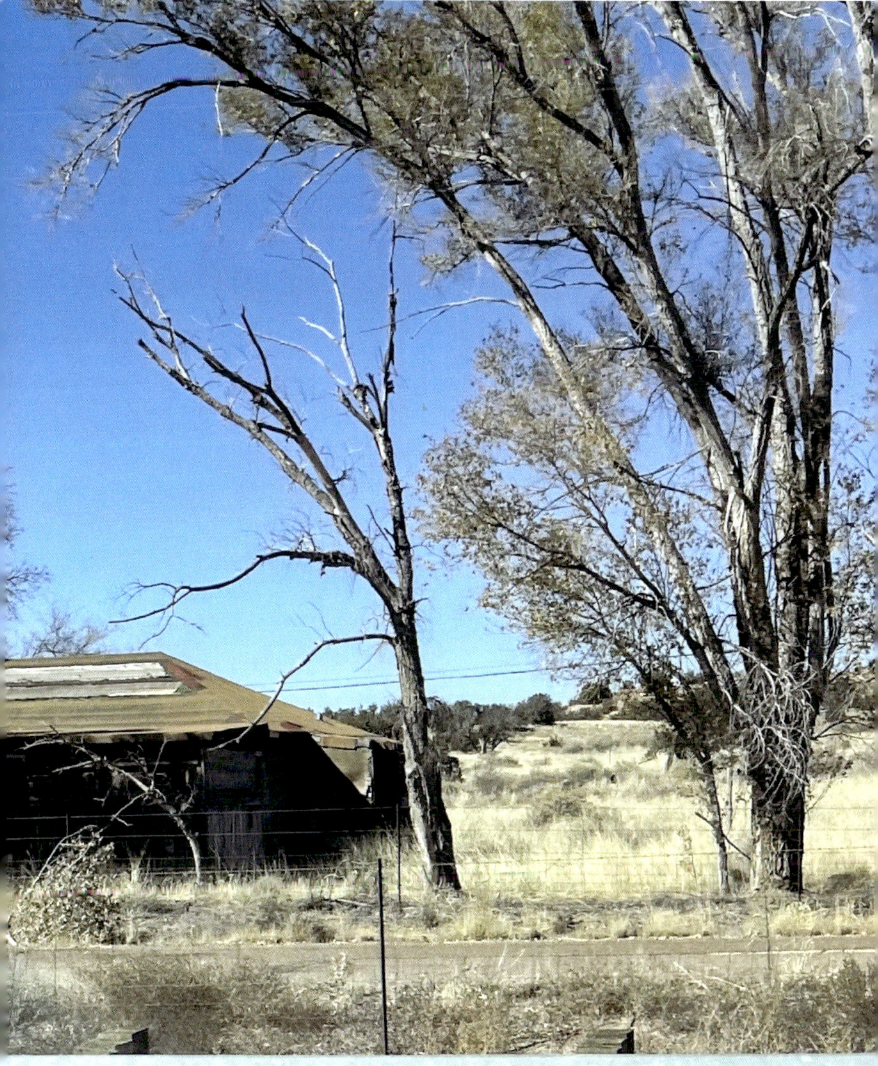

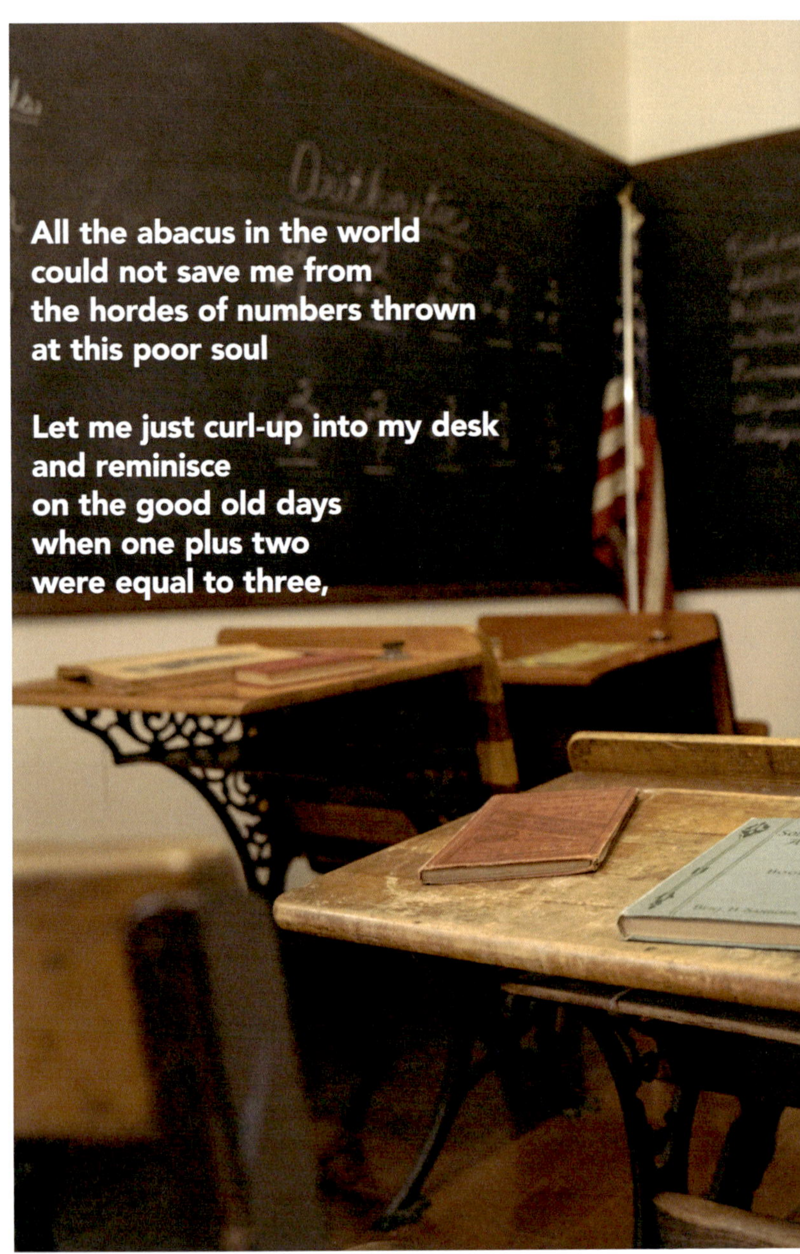

All the abacus in the world
could not save me from
the hordes of numbers thrown
at this poor soul

Let me just curl-up into my desk
and reminisce
on the good old days
when one plus two
were equal to three,

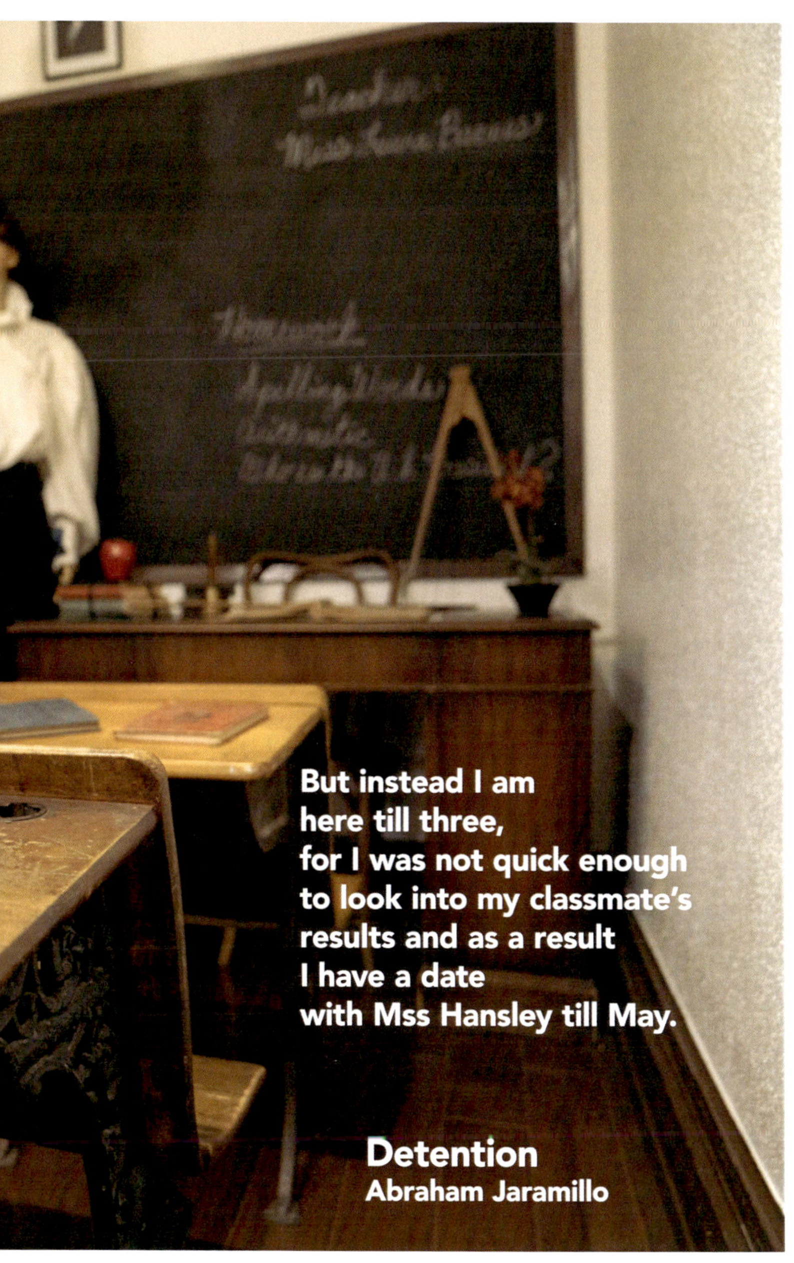

But instead I am
here till three,
for I was not quick enough
to look into my classmate's
results and as a result
I have a date
with Mss Hansley till May.

Detention
Abraham Jaramillo

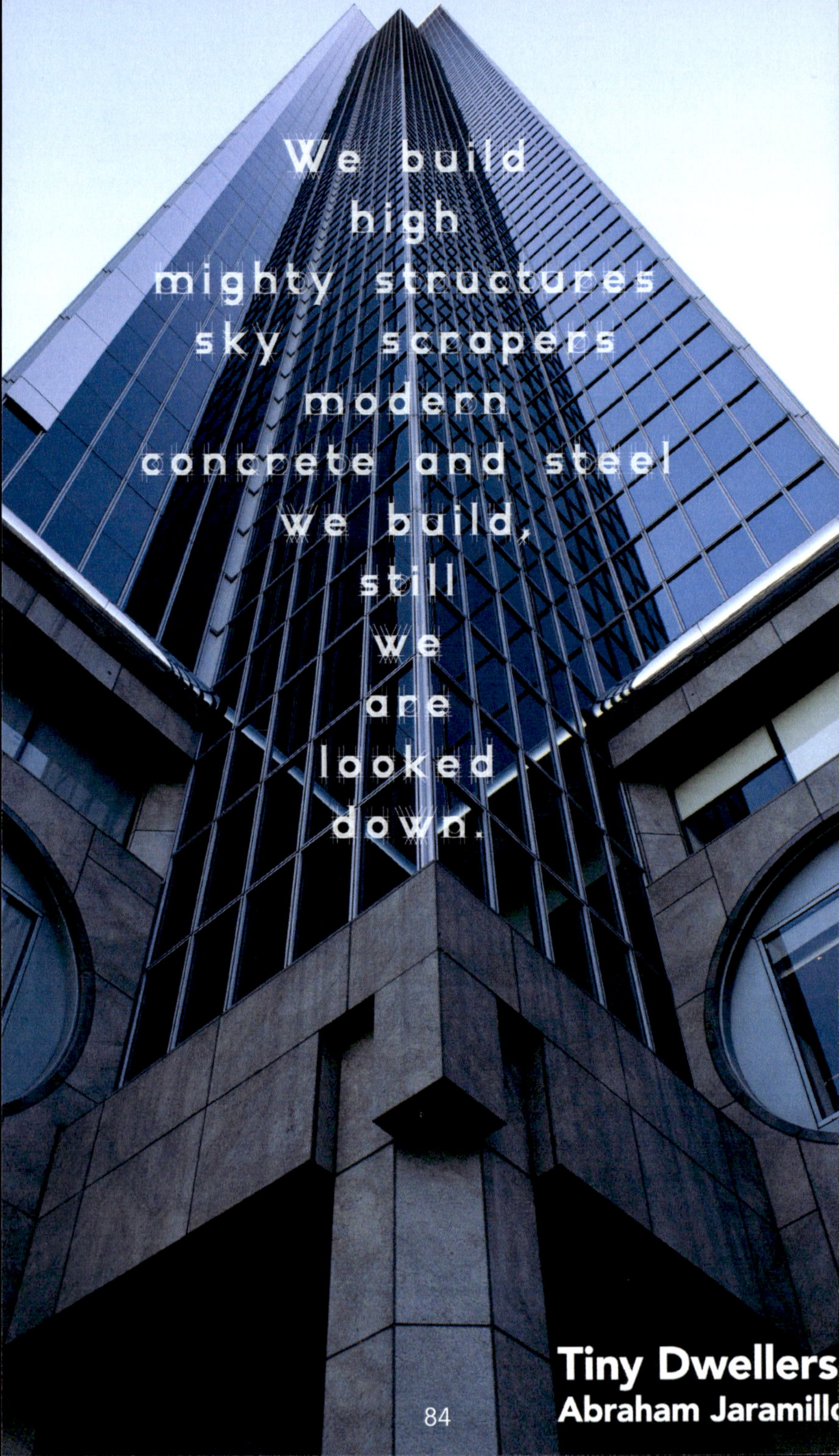

Tiny Dwellers

Abraham Jaramillo

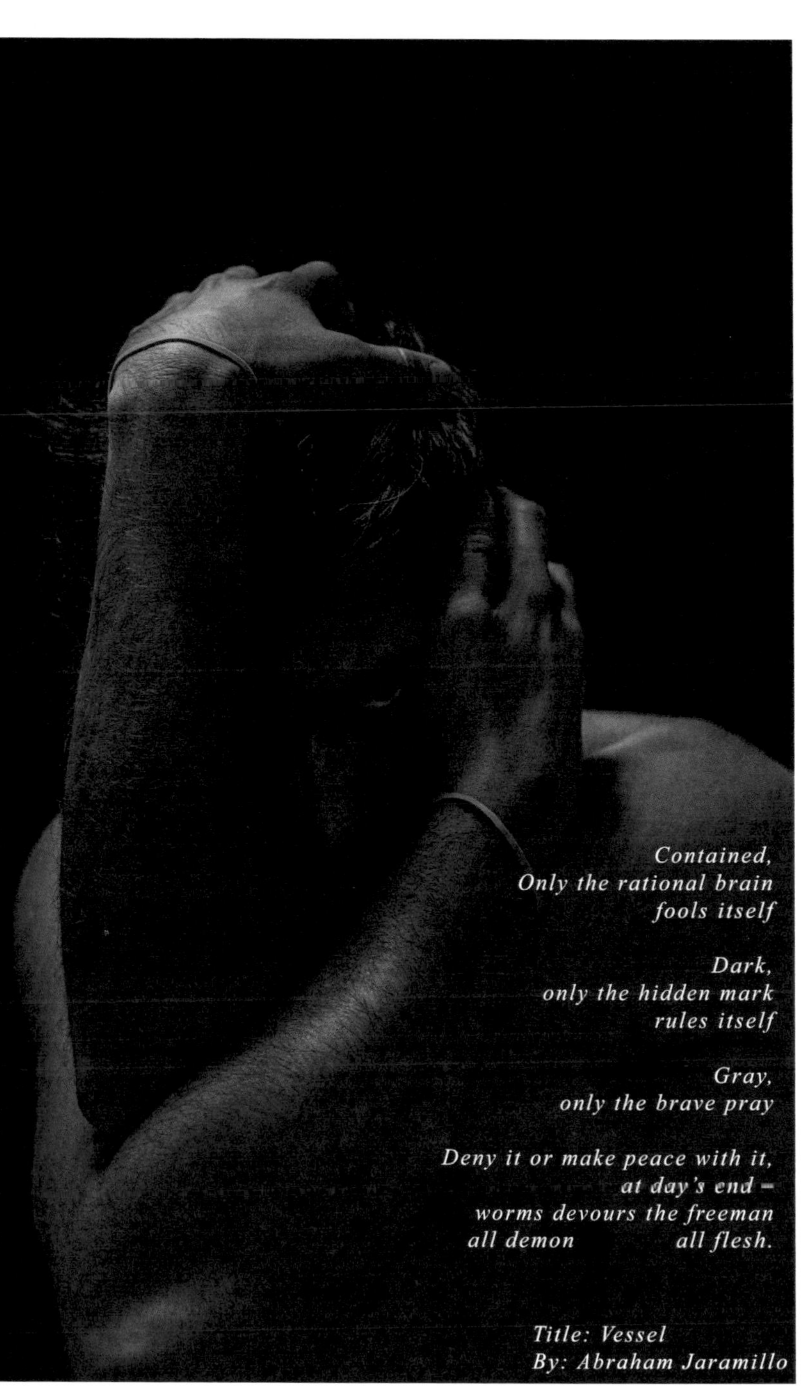

Contained,
Only the rational brain
fools itself

Dark,
only the hidden mark
rules itself

Gray,
only the brave pray

Deny it or make peace with it,
at day's end –
worms devours the freeman
all demon all flesh.

Title: Vessel
By: Abraham Jaramillo

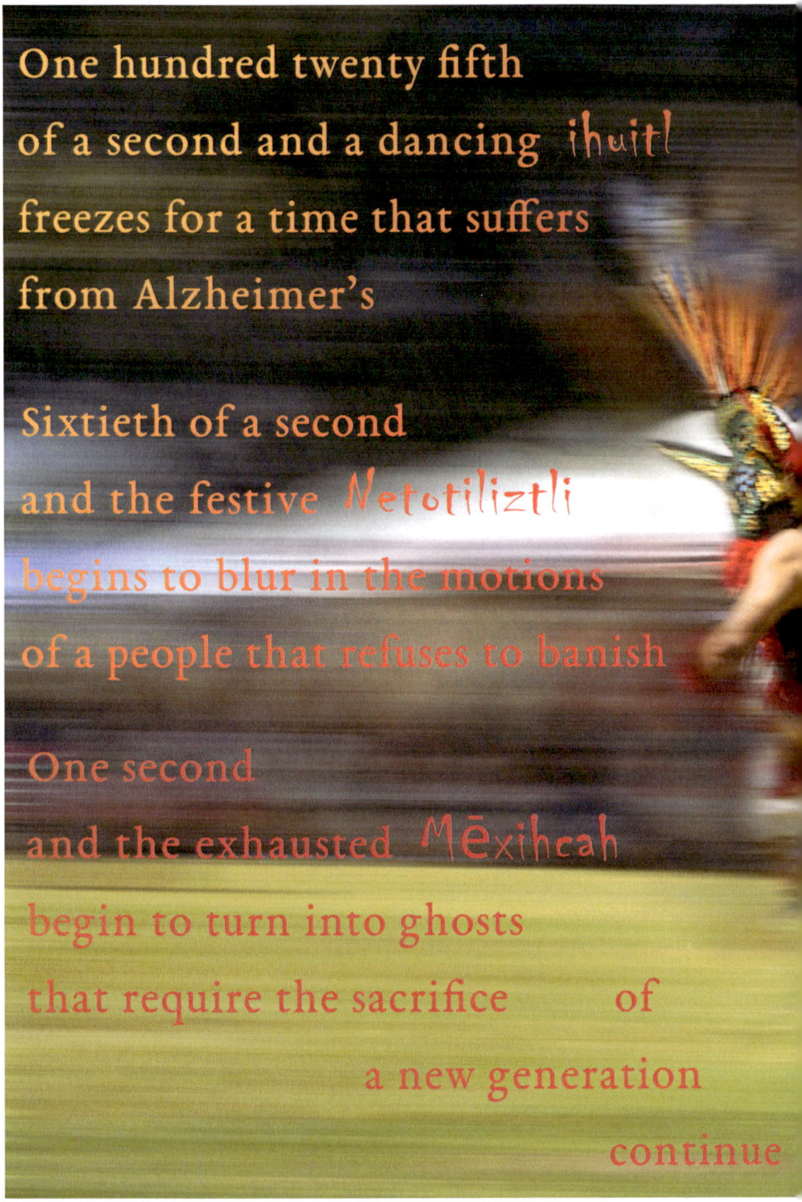

One hundred twenty fifth
of a second and a dancing ihuitl
freezes for a time that suffers
from Alzheimer's

Sixtieth of a second
and the festive Netotiliztli
begins to blur in the motions
of a people that refuses to banish

One second
and the exhausted Mēxihcah
begin to turn into ghosts
that require the sacrifice of
a new generation
continue

Ihuitl: pronunciation (EE-weetl), origin Náhuatl, meaning "feather"

Netotiliztli: pronunciation (ne-hto-tiliz- tli), origin Náhuatl, meaning "dance"

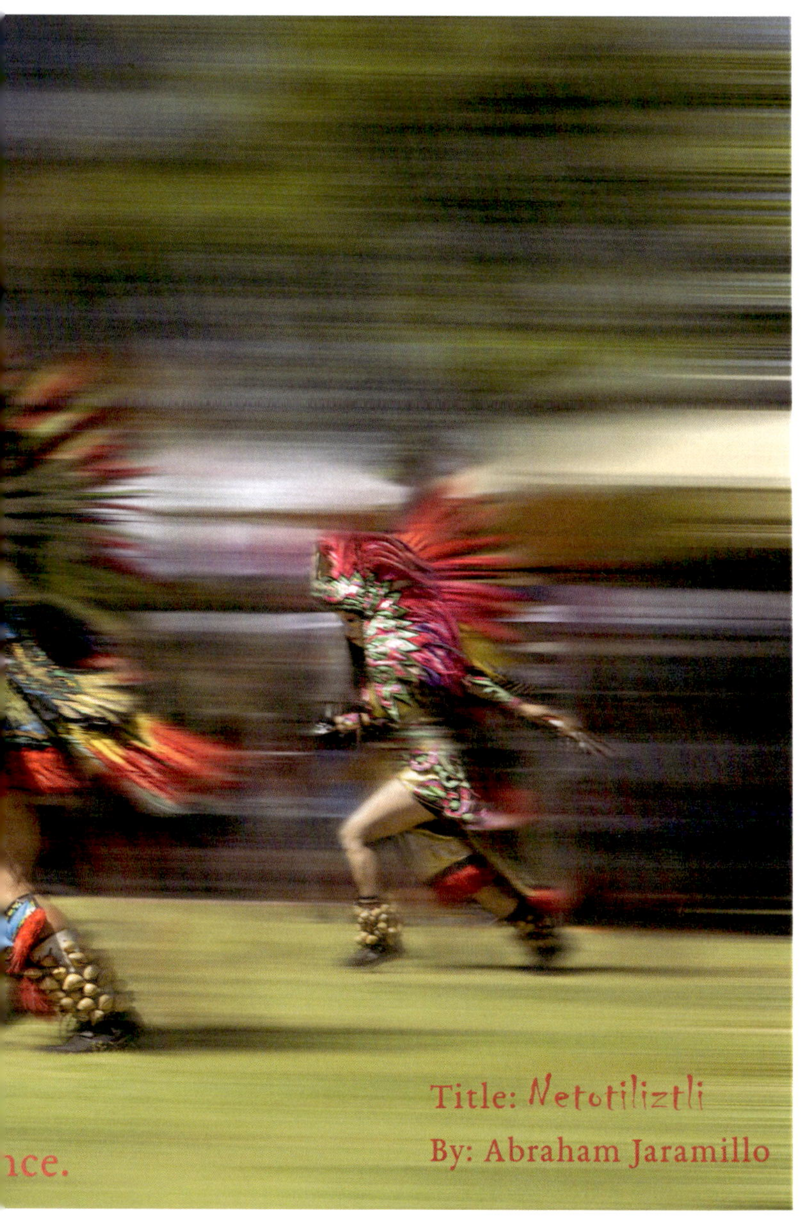

Mēxihcah: pronunciation (me-shi-kaa), origin Náhuatl, meaning "a Nahuatl-speaking people of the Valley of Mexico who were the rulers of the Triple Alliance, more commonly referred to as the Aztec Empire"

INTERRACIAL LOVINGS C

THIS GUARANTEE

I have examined the

of this card and find

moderate and free thin

with unusually strong

Color-blind LOVE possibil

well fitted to promot

freedom and future of in

relationships.

White Wash b

310-10.

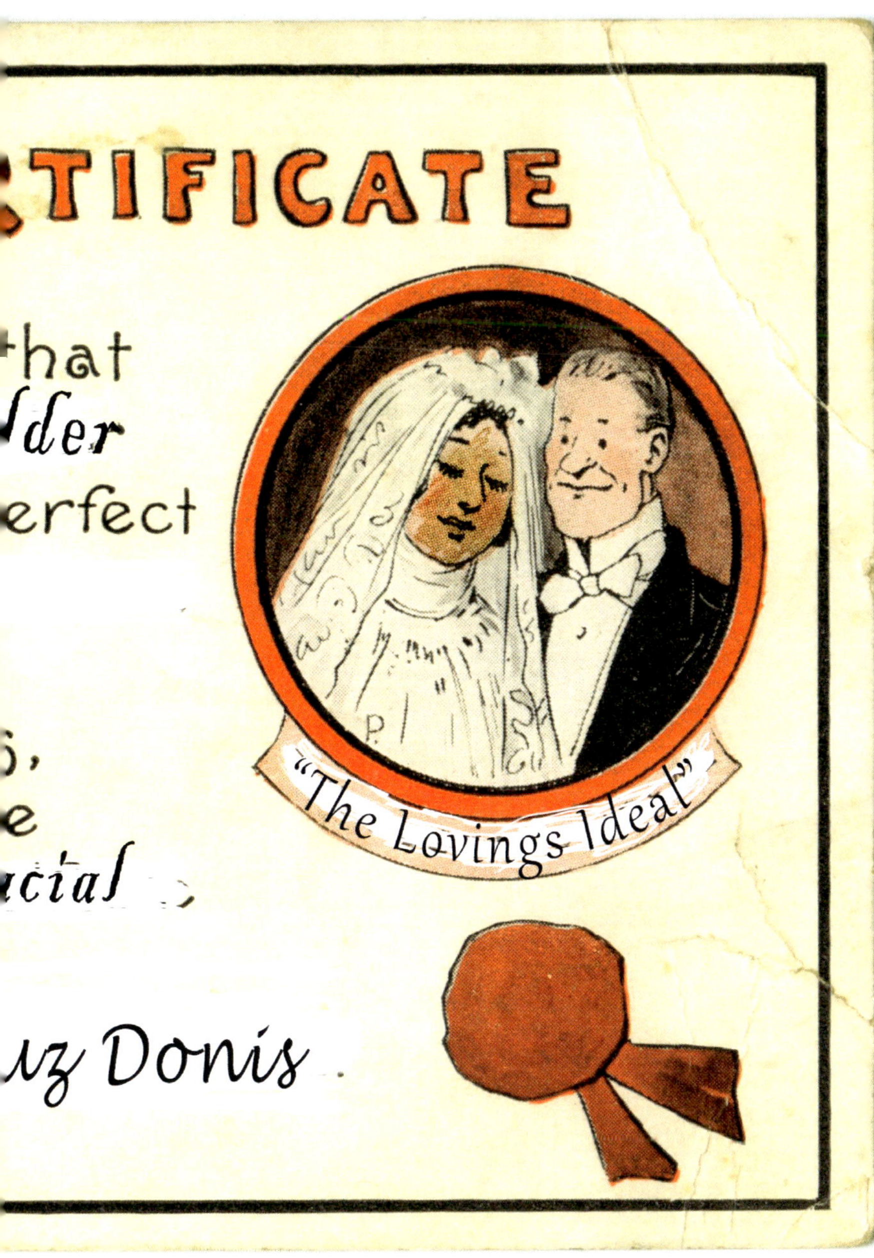
TIFICATE
that
lder
erfect
e
icial
iz Donis
"The Lovings Ideal"

About the Contributors
Sobre los Contribuidores

Clarissa Cervantes

Clarissa Cervantes is a travel/researcher/photographer. Clarissa's photo gallery includes images from all over the world where she finds inspiration to share her images with others through her creative lens, inviting the viewer to question, explore more, and look closer.

Alayna Abravanel

Alayna Abravanel joined our Conchas y Café workshop series after participating in our Journal of My Life series offered in partnership with the Los Angeles Public Library. Alayna tries to express herself in as many ways as she can.

Erica Castro

Erica Lopez is a veteran Xicana English teacher. She is currently in the book production of publishing "My Silent Voice Unleashed", "How to Find Peace through the Grieving Process", and "The Pieces Left Behind Poems". She participated in a suicide attempt survival collaboration called Alive to Thrive. Connect through *Instagram: @ericalopez74*

Nery Martinez Jr.

Finding pleasure in my writing, word by word, I found my truthful way. Playing the movie of my story since '93, born in Guatemala, spreading roots in LA.
@martinezjr.nery

Gabriela Martinez

My name is Gabriela Martinez and I love poetry. I have always found poetry to be so beautiful, almost like a slow song of some sort. I am a beginner and would love to share my poetry work with you all to enjoy!

Julie Rico

Julie Rico, from Detroit, Michigan, once worked on an assembly line, then at the World Headquarters of General Motors in Public Relations. She came to L.A. with a BA in Journalism. Julie works as a volunteer in Chinatown, L.A., as a writer and producer/manager of art projects.
facebook.com/juliericoartgallery
juilericogallery.com

T.D.M

An author with a passion for creating human experiences. T.D.M is a lifelong designer, creator, and photographer exploring different forms of creative expression hoping to make a positive impact in the world.

Marjan Modarres Sabzevari

Marjan Modarres Sabzevari is an Iranian, published translator, and photographer who graduated with a master's degree in English-Language Literature. Entering the 2016 Worldwide Photo Walk Leader Competition (Scott Kelby's), her photo was chosen as the elected one from Yazd.

Mojdeh Amini

Poetry is a rootless tool with endless loops to fool. The poet's intent is to give a different meaning to poetry.

River

River (They/them) is a US poet who encourages everyone to speak out against the active genocide occurring in Palestine. / River es un poeta estadounidense que fomenta a todos a hablar en contra del genocidio actual que está ocurriendo en Palestina.

Sanjuanita

Sanjuanita is an English and Spanish teacher at LAUSD. She has four grown-up kids. In her free time, she loves to read and write. She also likes the beach and spending time with her family. She also has two beautiful granddaughters! Oh, and she loves her dog Oreo!

Abraham Jaramillo

Planet Earth Artist, bound to create art that reflects nature, a range of human emotions, and a multitude of other topics using different types of media, such as poetry, photography, painting, etc. To discover more of his madness, follow him:

Instagram: @abraham_photoworld
www.a0jphotoworld.com

Luz Donis

Luz is a second generation Guatemalan, raised in Boyle Heights. She trained and worked as a nurse for L.A. County and L.A. Unified. She is currently immersed in Vipassana insight meditation, ceramics, and being a grandma.

About the Conchas y Café program

Conchas y Café is a 15-week workshop series for adults, focusing exclusively on creative writing, literacy, and illustration. Participants have the opportunity to work with volunteer writers and artists on developing artwork that will be published and presented in a biannual zine and public reading.

For more information, locations, and dates for upcoming Conchas y Café workshops, contact us by email at *info@DSTLArts.org*.

Acerca el programa Conchas y Café

Conchas y Café es un taller de 15 semanas para adultos, especializando en escritura, literatura, y dibujo. Participantes tienen la oportunidad de trabajar con escritores y artistas voluntarios en el desarrollo de obras de arte que serán publicados y presentados en publicaciones bianuales y lecturas públicas.

Para más información, localidades, y fechas de próximos talleres de Conchas y Café, contáctenos por correo electronico al *info@DSTLArts.org*.

This program is supported in part by:

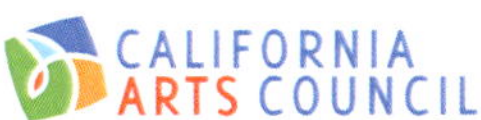

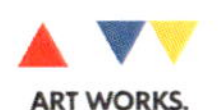

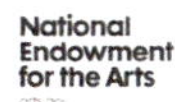

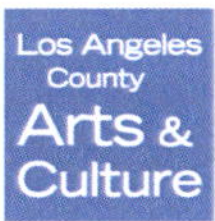

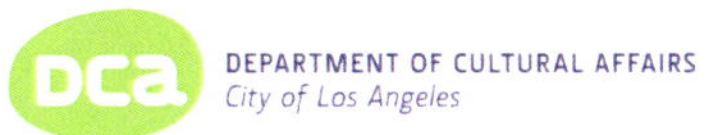

Previous Issues of *Conchas y Café Zine*:

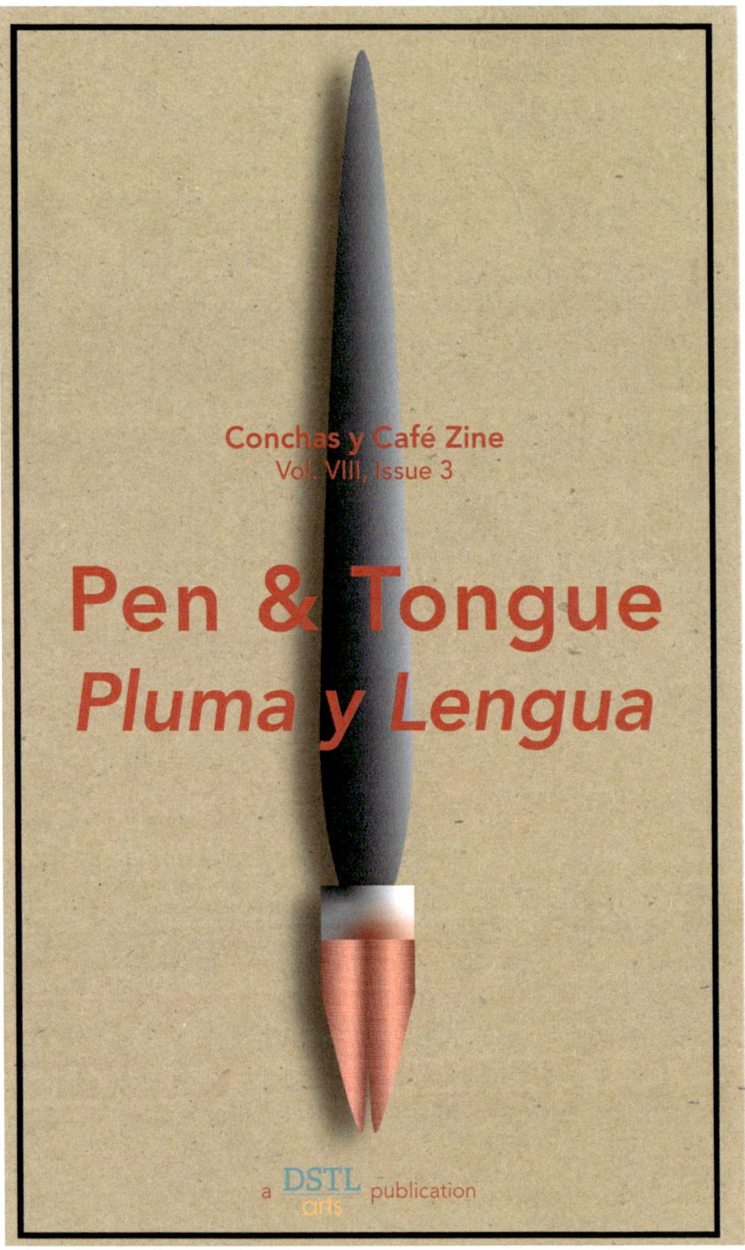

Pen & Tongue: Conchas y Café Zine; Vol. 8, Issue 3
available now at **DSTLArts.org/shop**

Previous Issues of *Conchas y Café Zine*:

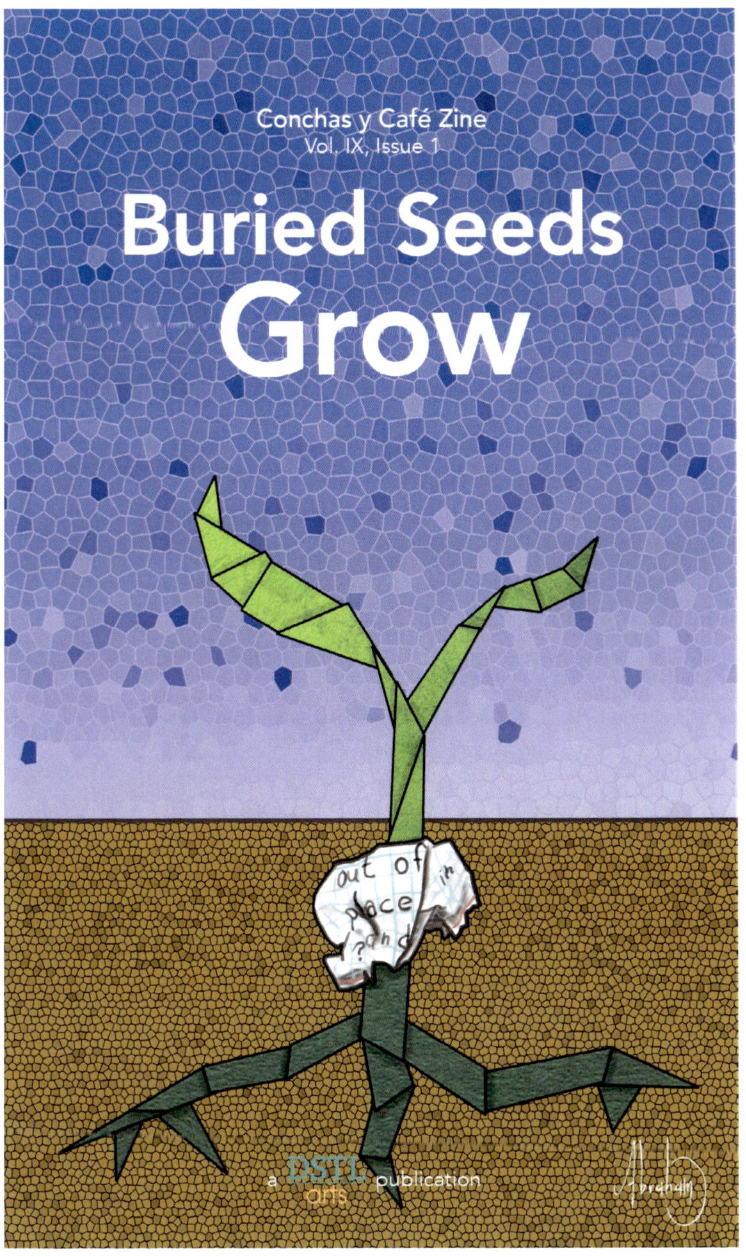

Buried Seeds Grow: Conchas y Café Zine; Vol. 9, Issue 1

available now at ***DSTLArts.org/shop***

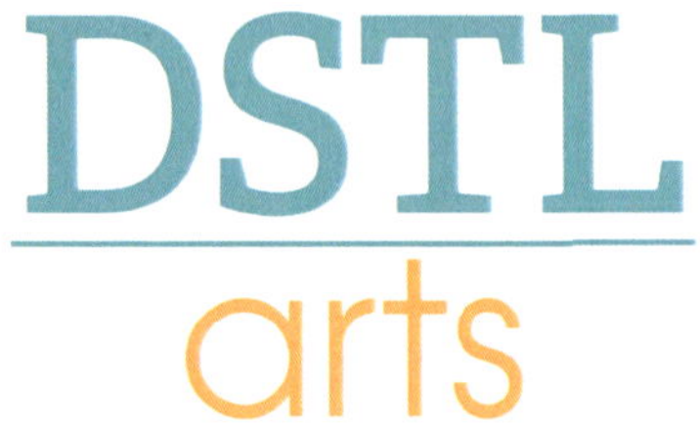

This publication was produced by DSTL Arts.

DSTL Arts is a nonprofit arts mentorship organization that inspires, teaches, and hires emerging artists from underserved communities.

To learn more about DSTL Arts, visit online at:

DSTLArts.org

@DSTLArts

www.ingramcontent.com/pod-product-compliance
Lightning Source LLC
LaVergne TN
LVRC090253110826
845147LV00007B/731

* 9 7 8 1 9 4 6 0 8 1 7 4 2 *